DRAMATISTS PLAY SERVICE

OUTSTANDING MEN'S MONOLOGUES

VOLUME TWO

Edited by CRAIG POSPISIL
with DANNA CALL

★

★

DRAMATISTS
PLAY SERVICE
INC.

OUTSTANDING MEN'S MONOLOGUES: VOLUME TWO
Copyright © 2010, Dramatists Play Service, Inc.

All Rights Reserved

INTRODUCTION

Several years ago I found myself in a theater bookstore looking at the large selection of monologue books. There were collections of all different stripes: comic monologues, dramatic monologues; monologues by women, by men; monologues collected by year; and many more. What caught my attention was that all of the collections included monologues from plays published by Dramatists Play Service where I work, and I thought, "Why not put together a monologue collection drawn solely from our plays?"

After all, Dramatists represents most of today's best playwrights, both exciting new authors just coming onto the scene, and well-established ones. We publish 41 plays that have won the Pulitzer Prize for Best Play and 27 that have won the Tony Award for Best Play.

So, I set about editing two collections of monologues from our recent plays, and *Outstanding Men's* and *Outstanding Women's Monologues* was born. Both collections were well received and quickly ran through their print runs. Now, with the invaluable editorial help and input of Danna Call, the series continues with *Outstanding Men's* and *Outstanding Women's Monologues: Volume Two.*

Each of these two new volumes contains over 50 monologues that we've selected from some of the exceptional plays published by Dramatists in the last several years. You'll find an enormous range of voices and subject matter, characters from their teens to their 60s, and authors of widely varied styles but all immensely talented.

Danna and I would particularly like to thank Diana Bedoya and Emily Kadish for their help in bringing these books to print.

We hope this new collection will be useful to you in finding new audition material, classroom work or just for the pleasure of reading. Perhaps you'll be introduced to some new authors as well. We know that you will find some very exciting writing for the theater in these pages.

Craig Pospisil
New York City

CONTENTS

100 SAINTS YOU SHOULD KNOW

BY KATE FODOR

MATTHEW — 30s

SYNOPSIS: Theresa is estranged from her family and working as a cleaning woman when she is surprised by the desire to learn how to pray. Matthew, the priest whose rectory she cleans, is stunned and heartbroken by the realization that he no longer knows how to talk to God. When Matthew disappears one day, Theresa feels compelled to track him down, and her search changes both of their lives.

TIME: The present.

(Out of the darkness, large black-and-white images appear, one by one. They are photographs: delicate gelatin silver prints of tall, pale, handsome men, completely naked. Below the pictures, Matthew is getting ready for bed. He has taken off his shoes and unbuttoned his shirt.)

MATTHEW. *(To the audience.)* These are the pictures that Mrs. Tierney, the church secretary, found in my study. They've given me three months to think about them. Three months to pray and to contemplate while a visiting priest from New Mexico tends to my congregation, and then I'm to meet with the bishop and explain myself. *(He looks at the pictures.)* They're by George Platt Lynes, a photographer who worked in New York City in the 1930s. He photographed movie stars for magazines, but he also took pictures — he also took pictures like these ones. I hadn't ever heard of him until I found a book called *George Platt Lynes* in the public library. I was looking in the L's in the art section for Lorenzo Lotto, who painted the lives of the saints on the walls of the Suardi chapel in Trescore in 1524, and I found *George Platt Lynes* instead. I don't think any patron of our local library had ever looked at the book before I did. The edge of each page peeled away from the next one as I turned it, the way they sometimes do in books that have never been read, as though you were breaking into something that's meant to stay sealed. *(A beat.)* I ripped the pictures out of the book. I took the book to a long table in the back of the library, away from the DVDs and the Internet access stations to a place in the library that's meant for reading and so is always utterly deserted, and I ripped out the pages I wanted. I don't know what came over me. I'm careful with books. I don't approve of dog-earing pages to mark your place. Not even that. And when I'm reading a book, I hold it open only three-quarters of the way, so as not to crack the binding. But I ripped out the pages and folded them into my pocket, and at home, I opened them and smoothed them with my hands. I think I took them because I felt somehow, just momentarily, at the quiet table in the library, that God was in the pictures. There is a line of thought that goes that beauty is God's goodness made visible, that it's in objects of beauty that we see the beauty of the Lord reflected. When God called me to service, he called me through beauty. In the church, there was incense and quiet. Dark wood. Masses and requiems. I went to talk to Father Michaels, and his study smelled of books, and bits of colored light from the stained-glass windows were thrown across the floor like someone had spilled a handful of rubies, and I thought, "For wisdom is better than rubies, and all the things that may be desired are not to be compared to it," and those words were my calling. So one can be called to God by beauty. But I know, also, now, that one can be called away from God by beauty. The Church teaches that as priests we are sanctified: that is, literally, separate, set apart for sacred use. I'm set apart. I'm set aside. I'm lonely. When I look at the pictures, I inhabit the bodies of the men; I don't look at them as objects of desire; I become them, just as a beginning step before even thinking about desire. I feel for the first time since I was a child what it might mean to have a body. Maybe even what it might mean to have a body in relation to another person's body. I look at the pictures, and those lines from St. John of the Cross come to me out of nowhere. "With his gentle hand he wounded my neck. And caused all my senses to be suspended." I didn't even know that I knew them, and suddenly they're all I can find in my head no matter what else I'm looking for. "Upon my flowery breast, Kept wholly for himself alone, There he stayed sleeping, and I caressed him." I know that it's supposed to be about God, but I just can't seem to hear it that way anymore. *(Blackout.)*

THE ACTION AGAINST SOL SCHUMANN

BY JEFFREY SWEET

AARON — Sol Schumann's adult son.

SYNOPSIS: Sol Schumann, a devout American Jew and beloved father of two grown sons, is accused of unspeakable crimes he allegedly committed many years earlier. The play tells of the bond that links parents and children and also of the gulf which separates them. Though Sol Schumann is the title character, the two central forces of the drama are his sons, who in the course of tracking through the maze of legal, moral and personal issues on the sins of their father, must also come to terms with their relationships with him as their father's children.

PLACE: New York City, Washington, D.C. and Toronto.

TIME: 1985.

(Aaron is having dinner with his brother Michael and friends Diane and Leah.)

AARON. I almost wanted to visit bayreuth. You know Bayreuth? Otherwise known as Wagner Central. Did you know that when he was a conductor — Wagner, I'm talking about — when he was assigned to conduct a score by a Jewish composer, he wore gloves? Yes. And after the piece was done, was finished, he'd throw the gloves away? But he manages to get this place built — Bayreuth — this huge opera house so they can stage his endless nutcase operas. So, years later: Hitler — big Wagner fan. During the war, Hitler keeps the place going full tilt — even when there are shortages 'cuz of the war — he thinks it's the beating heart of the German soul or something. Including in the orchestra, during the war, Jewish musicians. Yes, playing in the pit. Wrap your mind around that one. You're a Jewish oboe player, at the same time your relatives are being carted away, you're playing *Twilight of the Gods* for Der

Fuhrer. How honored they must have been by his applause. So —
this is the part I love — when American troops liberate the town,
some of the GIs look at this big opera palace and say, "Hey, cool
— a vaudeville house!" And they take it over and put up a show.
Every comic routine and number they can remember — the Marx
Brothers, the Ritz Brothers, Fanny Brice, Jack Benny, Danny Kaye.
Wagner's daughter-in-law hears about it, she nearly has a heart
attack. This vast, somber temple of high art being desecrated with
a bunch of jokes from kike comics. No, if there were any place in
Germany I'd actually want to visit, that would be it.

THE AGONY
& THE AGONY

BY NICKY SILVER

RICHARD AGLOW (pronounced AG-low, not a-GLOW) —
mid-40s. A once promising, now failed playwright. Articulate and
highly self-dramatizing.

*SYNOPSIS: Richard Aglow is a failure. A once-promising playwright,
he finds himself a virtual shut-in with only rejection letters to amuse
himself. Until today. He's started writing again! And as luck would
have it, inspiration has hit on the very day his wife, Lela, an aspiring
actress who married Richard despite his homosexuality, has met one of
New York's leading producers. This is Richard's chance, a golden opportunity to get back in the game. Of course, he'll have to overlook the fact
that the producer about to arrive is the man who wrote that last rejection, the one that broke Richard's spirit. The arrival of Lela's lover, his
pregnant girlfriend and the ghost of one of the twentieth century's most
notorious killers complicate matters further.*

PLACE: A lovely Upper West Side apartment.

TIME: Now.

RICHARD. I was twenty-one years old when I graduated from college and my parents gave me, as a gift, a week in London. This surprised me as the most extravagant gift I'd received before that were
some fish, when I was twelve, which died promptly from overfeed-
ing and were flushed, without ceremony after dinner one night. I
didn't take the trip until the following November and I was greeted
by grey skies and a small hotel room with fluorescent lights and two
twin beds, both of which had stains left by previous occupants.
[NATHAN. Is happy coming?]
RICHARD. Yes. I walked. That's all I did. All day and all night
and when I got hungry I ate at a fast food place which could easi-
ly have been right here, on any corner in any city, except for the

prices and the fact, of course, that diet Coke was called Coke Lite and everyone said "please" and "come again." On the fifth night of my visit. I was walking in one of those pedestrian cul-de-sacs that appear between buildings — and it started to snow. Not heavily — and there was no wind so the snow didn't sting. But perfectly, catching the light as each flake made its haphazard way to the ground. And then, from nowhere there was a man — I didn't see where he came from, but he was there and he was very beautiful, with light hair and a dark coat, and skin that you could tell was soft before you touched it. And when he spoke, I knew that he was foreign, Norwegian maybe, or a Dane. But here, now, on this British street, he was someone else, someone new, other than the person he had been all of his life ... So I was someone new. For two days, my last two days, I was someone else. And I was young and sure and sure of everything that was ahead of me ... and I was happy.

ALL THAT I WILL EVER BE

BY ALAN BALL

DWIGHT — A California surfer type pushing 30, kind of nerdy, kind of sexy.

SYNOPSIS: ALL THAT I WILL EVER BE is a darkly funny tale of cultural provocation and our eternal search for belonging as seen through the relationship of two young men in contemporary Los Angeles: Dwight, a privileged native Angeleno, and Omar, an enigmatic immigrant from the Middle East.

PLACE: Los Angeles, California.

TIME: The present.

(A car. Dwight drives; Omar sits beside him, staring out the window.)

DWIGHT. I can't decide which was worse — the queeny British guy who sold nuclear secrets, or the eyeliner on all the Romanian terrorists. Can you believe they still use that fucking Eisenhower-era code to make the bad guys not just bad, but really like, disgusting and filthy and depraved? As if plotting the slaughter of millions of people wasn't bad enough. (Omar keeps staring out the window, preoccupied. Troubled.) But at the same time, the one woman? The only woman in the entire fucking film? Turns out to be a suicide bomber? (Shakes his head.) I mean, think about the message of this movie: Women are apocalyptic bitches that cannot be trusted, foreign faggots are deviant evil fucks who want to kill the whole world, but the love of one hot American soldier for another hot American soldier is pure, and noble, and tragic ... and all that erotic tension between men, my God, it's like they have to destroy entire cities just to keep from fucking each other —
[OMAR. (Quietly.) Jesus. It's just a movie.]
DWIGHT. It's not just a movie. It's mythology. People all over the world are going to go see it, and all that bizarre subtextural anxiety about male sexuality is going to get imprinted on millions of minds

13

worldwide —
[OMAR. *You're making a molehill out of a mountain.*]
DWIGHT. Sometimes, I really do think, if men everywhere would just fuck each other, we would have no war.

ALL THE RAGE

BY KEITH REDDIN

CHRIS — Depressed man in his 20s/30s.

SYNOPSIS: A blood-splattered body lies on the living room carpet at the start of ALL THE RAGE, and by the end of this dark comic examination of our culture of violence, eleven characters have been killed, sent to prison or gone mad. The action takes place in an unnamed city today, in a series of scenes that show the interconnected lives of ten characters. A modern-day Jacobean revenge tragedy, ALL THE RAGE gives us a picture of a world spinning out of control, as everybody has a gun and is ready to use it.

CHRIS. Doctor Gadney killed love for me. *[...]* He killed love. He made me see that nothing mattered, because there was a reason for everything. I was insecure because my mother didn't pay enough attention to me, and my father drank, and my brother went to prison for insider trading because, you see, he was trying to get acknowledgement from my father who ignored him as a child, so everything was okay. Adultery and murder and lying and cheating, it was all caused by some inner child crying for attention and if we recognized that child it was permissible. And how can love exist in Gadney's world, which became my world? Love I would think requires selflessness. Also Doctor Gadney prescribed Prozac.
[TENNEL. Ah.]
CHRIS. Made me want to suck the exhaust pipe every morning.
[TENNEL. And now?]
CHRIS. Now I get by without love. I try to be comfortable. But even that eludes me. I thought try for comfort. Comfort isn't Peace or Love or anything that starts with a capital letter. Comfort is a nice place to live and cable; maybe dinner out once in awhile. Thought if I hooked up with someone made a lot of money, it wouldn't be love but it might bring comfort. Even that's worn out. So I think about the Prozac. That keeps me focused. Focused on killing myself, but focused.
[TENNEL. Oh dear.]
CHRIS. I'm not depressing you am I?

ALMOST BLUE

BY KEITH REDDIN

PHIL — A loner, 30s/40s.

SYNOPSIS: ALMOST BLUE is a stage noir set in a seedy rooming house, whose tenants include a man just out of prison trying to stay straight, a strange loner down the hall who writes pornographic greeting cards, a violent ex-con who wants to settle old scores and, of course, a beautiful woman in trouble, who messes with everybody's head. Written in a series of brutal, funny encounters, ALMOST BLUE is a journey into the dark night, full of plot twists and sultry exchanges.

PHIL. *(Pause.)* I'll tell you the dream I had last night. It was easy to remember. I have the same dream every night. I've had this dream for years and years, always the same dream. I've tried to have other dreams, but it's always the same.

In this dream I'm a much younger man. I have my whole life in front of me. I meet a woman, I fall in love with her. But deep down inside I know she doesn't love me the same way. I don't want to admit it to myself, but I know it's true. I know she sometimes sleeps with other men. I can never prove this, I don't have to, but I know it's true. And she knows I know. One day she tells me she's pregnant, that we're going to have a baby. I don't care that the baby might not be mine, I love this woman so very much, I'll love the baby, I'll love and take care of this baby we are going to have. In the dream we have the baby, it's a girl. I have this beautiful daughter, I love her, I love her even more than my wife, if that's possible. And years go by and things aren't great but I try to be a good husband and a good father and I care for the daughter even though my wife is away from us for longer and longer periods of time. One time she's gone for a week. Just like that she leaves and is gone for a week and then comes back, and we don't talk about it, because we know if we say anything, we will break the spell, the spell that keeps everything together. But the spell is broken. She tells me she's leaving. She never loved me, and now she's going and she doesn't want our daughter, she hates it and she hates me and she wishes we both would die and then she walks

16

out the door and she's gone.

But the dream doesn't end there. No, it keeps going. In the dream, I'm now alone in my room with my daughter and I say to her everything's going to be okay. Mommy's going away on a trip but it's going to be alright, we'll do fine on our own. But it isn't alright and weeks go by and months and things only get worse, and one evening I take a lot of sleeping pills and I grind them up and put them in a sandwich, I give them to my daughter and she eats them like the good girl she is and she gets sleepy and I say let's have a bath and then we'll put you to bed, shall we?

And I run a bath and I put my daughter in the water and then I push her head under the water and I hold her and hold her and she starts thrashing about and splashing water everywhere and I hold her and I hold her and then she stops and all the air goes out of her and she's dead and I dress her and put her on the bed and then I go downstairs and take the rest of the pills and lay down next to my daughter and wait to die.

But I don't die, I just get sick, really sick and I start to vomit and I call the police and tell them to send an ambulance. And when they get to my house they come upstairs and I say, I'm sorry I think something terrible has happened.

The last part of the dream happens very fast. In the dream I'm put on trial and I plead guilty, guilty as charged and I'm sent to prison for life, only they let me out after twelve years. They tell me I'm ready to rejoin society, I've paid my debt, I'm a free man. And I leave the prison and find a room and sit on my bed in the dark and stare at the wall. And then I wake up. *(Pause.)* What do you think of my dream?

ANNA IN THE TROPICS

BY NILO CRUZ

JUAN JULIAN — The lector, 38.

SYNOPSIS: ANNA IN THE TROPICS is set in a Cuban-American cigar factory in Florida in 1929, when cigars were still rolled by hand and "lectors" were employed to educate and entertain the workers. The arrival of a new lector is a cause for celebration, but when he begins to read aloud from Anna Karenina, *he unwittingly becomes a catalyst in the lives of his avid listeners, for whom Tolstoy, the tropics and the American dream prove a volatile combination.*

PLACE: An old warehouse. Tampa, Florida. A small town called Ybor City.

TIME: 1929.

JUAN JULIAN. Señor Chester, allow me to say something. My father used to say that the tradition of having readers in the factories goes back to the Taino Indians. He used to say that tobacco leaves whisper the language of the sky. And that's because through the language of cigar smoke the Indians used to communicate to the gods. Obviously I'm not an Indian, but as a lector I am a distant relative of the Cacique, the Chief Indian, who used to translate the sacred words of the deities. The workers are the *oidores*. The ones who listen quietly, the same way Taino Indians used to listen. And this is the tradition that you're trying to destroy with your machine. Instead of promoting and popularizing machines, why don't you advertise our cigars? Or are you working for the machine industry? *[OFELIA. He's right. We need more advertising, so we can sell more cigars.]*
JUAN JULIAN. Let's face it, Chester, workers, cigars aren't popular anymore. Moving pictures now feature their stars smoking cigarettes: Valentino, Douglas Fairbanks ... They are all smoking little fags and not cigars. You can go to Hollywood and offer our cigars to producers. *[CHECHÉ. You're being cynical ...]*

18

JUAN JULIAN. No, I'm warning you. This fast mode of living with machines and moving cars affects cigar consumption. And do you want to know why, Señor Chester? Because people prefer a quick smoke, the kind you get from a cigarette. The truth is that machines, cars, are keeping us from taking walks and sitting on park benches, smoking a cigar slowly and calmly. The way they should be smoked. So you see, Chester, you want modernity, and modernity is actually destroying our very own industry. The very act of smoking a cigar.

BEAUTIFUL CHILD

BY NICKY SILVER

HARRY — Isaac's father.

SYNOPSIS: Can we love someone who falls outside our moral code? BEAUTIFUL CHILD presents Harry and Nan, a couple whose marriage has become a comfortable battleground of witty barbs and infidelity. Everything they think they know, however, is called into question when their son, Isaac, an art teacher and painter, comes for lunch and asks if he can stay. The world's no longer safe for Isaac, as his secrets are about to become public — he has fallen in love, and has been having an affair, with one of his students, an eight-year-old boy named Brian. Harry and Nan search for clues, desperate to make sense of this horror, alternately looking for exoneration and punishment for what must be their fault. They want to help their son, and they want to love him. But how? And what is their responsibility to the world and to the children in Isaac's future?

PLACE: The living room of an elegant home and a section of patio.

TIME: The present.

HARRY. This was my child. When Isaac was seventeen I drove him to college. I remember the day. Nan didn't come, she wasn't feeling well — or maybe she just said she wasn't because it was clear that he didn't want her. Of course he didn't want me either, but it was my car and there was luggage and I was driving. So he pretended he was happy. And I pretended I was happy. And he pretended he believed me and on and on and on — like looking at yourself, standing between mirrors. And we listened to the radio because we didn't know what to say. I made early attempts, but the fact is "Are you nervous?" and "Do you need any money?" sounded like Spanish — All the words just stayed in the air, piling up until I couldn't see the windshield. I left him, my son, in his room, in the dorm, with his roommate, a sad young man who returned my smile with a grimace, and I knew that it was time for me to leave. I walked out, through the building, through the rooms, through the air, to my car and I never looked back, because I knew, somehow, that it was over. I knew, that day, that my child was gone … I was wrong. He was gone, I think, years ago, years before. He was gone when he was here, in his room, in the yard. He was already gone. I should've looked back.

BLACK SHEEP

BY LEE BLESSING

CARL WINSHIP — 26, a black sheep. Carl is black; the others are white.

SYNOPSIS: A prominent family's "black sheep" nephew, Carl, the product of an interracial marriage, comes to stay with them after being released from prison. But does the family want him? And what does he want from them? In this dark comedy issues of race, sex and family values play out with wildly comic and disturbing results.

TIME: The present.

(As scene shifts, Max enters and freezes, looking across the lake with a pair of binoculars.)

CARL. *(To audience, contemplating first Max, then the lake.)* I always loved this lake. When I was little, Max and I used to swim in it. No one could understand why we wanted to swim in the lake. The pool was right here. But there was this rock formation in the lake, just under the surface and a deep spot — not bad, maybe ten feet deep — on the far side of it. We knew we shouldn't go near it. The rocks were too smooth to get back up. Neither of us could swim for shit, but I pretended I could. *(As Max slowly lowers his binoculars and continues to stare out over the lake.)* It really pissed Max off. He could see already that I was going to turn out a hell of a lot better than him. I'd catch him every once in awhile, rubbing his arm, staring at his skin. I knew what he was thinking: "At least I have this." *(As Max slowly raises the binoculars again and looks through them across the lake.)* One time I slipped and went straight down into that hole. I couldn't get to the surface. Max was on top of the rock, staring down at me. All he had to do was reach down and pull me up. And he did, of course. But not before he watched me. Not before he watched that little black boy waving helplessly in the water, panicked, clawing at the mossy stone, knowing he was going to die.

22

BOYS AND GIRLS

BY TOM DONAGHY

JASON — Early 30s.

SYNOPSIS: BOYS AND GIRLS is a contemporary look at family. Two couples in their early thirties, with a complicated history of love and loss, reach across vast obstacles in order to grow up, settle down and raise a child. But not necessarily in that order.

(Reed returns home and lies down on his bed. His eyes are shut only a moment when Jason enters the room. Reed sits up, not knowing what to say. Jason paces before beginning.)

JASON. You can't do that. You can't anymore. Calling me. And some set place. Some agreement we come to and showing up at a certain time only to — to — you can't. That's it. I don't want the keys anymore. *(He throws a set of keys on the floor.)* It's too easy. It's this thing that we should be sure we're thinking. I don't want to be in intimate situations and not have thought behind them. Not be conscious, not consciously know what we're doing. And fuck you! Fuck me? Fuck you! I am fine. I'm fine. I'm sitting there fine at my desk and you call and make plans?! Fuck you. Like nothing's happened. Six months now! Something's happened and fuck you. Everyone knows. My friends say this is nothing. No reason at all. You overreacted and then, what, I have to come meet you in some place you've found in what, Zagat's? And sit there and eat hummus? I don't like hummus, it dries me out! And I'm meeting you places like we're still together when we are not. And getting into this whole thing that you start — and I'm just getting clear in my head — you know — and every time I start to get clear you call me up. And I don't call you — you call me. I'm sitting there fine, at my desk doing well. Everyone there says my work is excellent. That's what they say and you call me. You call me …
[REED. (Beat.) I didn't mean to. (Beat.) I just wanted to see you.]
JASON. You shit. What about me? Those shirts, that closet full of shirts for who? No one else likes them. You're the only one who

likes me in blues and purples!

[REED. I'm sorry.]

JASON. Shut up.]

[REED. You can say that.]

JASON. Shut up, shut up. *(Jason reaches for Reed's hand. He then sits next to Reed on the bed.)* I don't want any of those pictures. Don't make copies for me. Vieques — I picked out the ones I like. That time in Atlanta, or upstate. Anything. Any of that. You know I don't collect things. I've left boxes everywhere and I forget what's in them and I never need them again. So don't track me down with souvenirs. Sentimental little kitschy little maudlin little things. That stuffed thing with the key chain, I don't need that. I've taken everything I need to take. If you, in the next months, a book, something turns up — I don't care. Salvation Army. Poor people can have those things. Give anything you find that's mine to someone who wants it. I don't. Things don't matter to me.

BUG

BY TRACY LETTS

PETER — 20s.

SYNOPSIS: Set in a seedy Oklahoma City motel room, the play cen-ters on the meeting between Agnes, a divorced waitress with a fondness for cocaine and isolation, and Peter, a soft-spoken Gulf War drifter introduced to her by her lesbian friend, R.C. Agnes stays at the motel hoping to avoid her physically abusive ex-husband, Jerry, newly released from prison. At first, she lets Peter sleep on her floor, but soon promotes him to the bed. Matters become more complicated as Jerry eagerly returns, expecting to resume their relationship. On top of that, a hidden bug infestation problem has both Agnes and Peter dealing with scathing welts and festering sores — which Peter believes are the result of experiments conducted on him during his stay at an army hos-pital. Their fears soon escalate to paranoia, conspiracy theories and twisted psychological motives.

PLACE: A motel room on the outskirts of Oklahoma City.

TIME: The present.

PETER. I got in some trouble ... with the Army. I was stationed at Sakaka ... the Syrian Desert, during the war. The doctors came in and really worked us over, with shots and pills, ostensibly for inoculation, but ... there was something else going on, too. A lot of the guys got sick, vomiting and diarrhea, migraines, blackouts. One guy had an epileptic seizure; he'd never had one before. A cou-ple of guys went AWOL. I never found out what really happened to them. I started having weird thoughts, too, and feeling ... sick. They shipped me home, put me in a hospital at Groom Lake. They started running these tests. They had every kind of doctor you could imagine, probing at me, jabbing me, asking me all kinds of weird questions, feeding me more pills. They wouldn't let me go. They kept me there — years, I don't know, four years? Those fuck-ing doctors were experimenting on me.

I went AWOL. I was a lifer, too. I didn't have anywhere to go. They don't respond too well to some drugged-up guinea pig just taking off. I don't know that I'm not carrying some disease with me, some contagion. Jesus, you know that's how they start, typhoid, Legionnaires' disease, some government screw-up, AIDS with those fucking monkeys in Africa. They're after me. These people don't fuck around, Agnes.

I shouldn't have told you that. But I needed to tell somebody. And I do trust you. I don't think you're just some simpleton I can take advantage of. I know we haven't known each other very long, but ... I like you, Agnes. I don't want to go ... I don't want to go ...

COMPLEAT FEMALE STAGE BEAUTY

BY JEFFREY HATCHER

CHARLES II — 32. The King.

SYNPOSIS: In 1661, the most famous portrayer of female roles on the London stage was a performer named "Kynaston." Like every other player permitted to enact such roles, Kynaston was a man. Ned or Mr. K, as he's called, is applauded onstage and off for his interpretations of Shakespeare's tragic ladies. He's the toast of the town and the very secret "mistress" of the powerful Duke of Buckingham. But when an unknown named Margaret Hughes plays Desdemona one night at an illegal theater, instead of stopping the show, the ever-game King Charles II changes the law to allow women to act. By the stroke of a pen, Kynaston's world is turned upside down, and such women as the king's own courtesan, Nell Gwynn, and Kynaston's former dresser, Maria, become stars.

PLACE: London.

TIME: 1660s.

CHARLES II. Kynaston! *[…]* You're talking about the Law. My Law. Twenty years ago, it was illegal for a woman to act onstage … in public. But in the palace … women galore! Private musicals, masques, no one gave a damn! Except the clerics. One minister, Mr. Prynne, wrote a pamphlet against all actresses as lewd women and whores. My mother acted in some of those court masques. She felt Mr. Prynne's diatribe was directed at her. So Mr. Prynne was tried, convicted, and sentenced to the stocks where his feet were burned, his ears lopped off, and his tongue cut out. Still, Mr. Prynne never recanted. Some say his stoicism in the face of such "excess" is what fanned the flames of the Puritan revolt. And so off with my father's head, and I to Holland for twenty years. Exile is a dreadful thing for one who knows where is his rightful place. *(Beat.)* I changed the law because it was time for a change; balance the scales, give the girls a chance. If the public rebels, they'll clamor for your return. I shall listen for that clamor, and when that clamor comes, the bells will ring your repeal. But I haven't heard a tinkle yet. Besides, it's a sop to the Church. The priests always preached against boys playing women, said it led to effeminacy and sodomy. Well, they're priests, they'd know. So we say, "There! See? New Law. No more boys in dresses! Just girls flashing tits! Happy now?"

DEDICATION OR THE STUFF OF DREAMS

BY TERRENCE McNALLY

LOU NUNCLE — 40s/early 50s.

SYNOPSIS: Lou and Jessie Nuncle run a children's theatre in a mall in upstate New York. With the possibility of taking over an abandoned vaudeville palace, the Nuncles are forced to examine how far their love of theatre will take them.

PLACE: A theatre.

TIME: Now.

LOU. So, here I am, center stage, solus, on a real stage in a real theatre. A stage and theatre that by rights should belong to me and not some alcoholic millionaire who is letting it go beyond all repair or reason. By what rights is it mine? Divine rights, artistic rights, moral ones. Not that they count for much in these impoverished times when wealth equals good and big equals better. I would transform this shabby, forgotten, forlorn room into a place of wonder and imagination again. That chandelier would sparkle anew if I had to polish every crystal myself. The aisles would be newly carpeted in a gesture of welcome and respect. Those rows of broken seats would be reclaimed in a plush red velvet that said, "Sit down, children, you are safe here. We are going to take you on a wonderful journey to China or Persia or Timbuktu." Today we are going to tell you the amazing story of your favorite character, anyone you choose. But before we begin, there are a few rules, so listen up. I said listen up, you kids in the balcony. That means you, too. No kicking the seat in front of you. No paper airplanes or spitballs. No putting chewing gum under the arms or seat of your chair. No talking, unless the action becomes so unbearably exciting that you have to call out: "Turn around, Robin Hood, quick, the Sheriff is going to kill you." Or so sad that you won't be able to live if you don't speak up. It's up to you that Tinker Bell doesn't die, that Abraham doesn't sacrifice his firstborn. For the precious time that you are here and we actors are before you, the future of the world is in your hands, the fate of the human race is yours to decide. Think about it. The possibilities are boundless, the responsibility is yours. And don't forget to breathe! I know, we all forget to sometimes in the theatre. Me, too. I also stop breathing, it's so wonderful. *(He takes in a deep breath, then lets it out.)* And always the curtain will fall, the story will have ended, and we actors will take our bows. Houselights up! It's over. We can all go home now. But something has changed. Tinker Bell has lived. Cinderella has found her Prince. You will go back to your real world and it will still be raw and painful, ugly even, but maybe a little less so because of what you have seen here today. Harmony and happiness were possible. And I will go back to my real world and it, too, will be a little more bearable, a little less unbearable because of what I have given you — and in giving you, have given myself: love and laughter, which are a good deal more nourishing at your age than bread and games. Hell, at any age. You lucky, lucky children. When I was your age, I didn't have a theatre in my life. I had to invent one of my own. All I had was a mirror, my mother's closet, and my music. *(Strains of Tchaikovsky's* Sleeping Beauty.*)* I'm telling you a secret now. A secret no one knows but you — not even Jessie, and I tell her every-thing. Well, almost everything. I would go to my mother's closet and take out her fullest skirt. I would put on the music I loved the best, the *Sleeping Beauty* — it was a waltz — and start to twirl in front of the mirror. Slow, slow I'd twirl, in-a-trance-kind-of slow. For hours sometimes. It felt like forever.

DEN OF THIEVES

BY STEPHEN ADLY GUIRGIS

FLACO — Late 20s/early 30s.

SYNOPSIS: Maggie is a junk-food-binging shoplifter looking to change her life. Paul is her formerly 400-pound compulsive-overeating sponsor in a twelve-step program for recovering thieves. Flaco, Maggie's jealous ex-boyfriend, is a charismatic wannabe Puerto Rican, small-time thief, who spins a grammatically challenged but persuasive yarn about $750,000 in unprotected drug money sitting in a safe in a downtown disco. This would-be criminal crew is rounded out by Flaco's new girlfriend, Boochie — a malaprop-slinging topless dancer. When things don't go according to plan, this hapless quartet finds themselves at the mercy of Louie "The Little Tuna" Pescatore, a reluctant heir to the criminal empire run by his father — "The Big Tuna" — who has left him in charge for the weekend. The penalty for stealing from the Tuna is death. But Louie offers them a break: "I need one body and three thumbs, you can choose the who, whys and wherefores among yourselves." Tied to chairs and able to move only their mouths, they must now fight for their lives by out-arguing each other as to who deserves to live.

FLACO.   Check this out: my friend, Raheem, right? He got a friend, who got a friend, who sell crack to this punk who works at this club, right? It's a big fuckin' disco called Epiphany. So I go down there, right, to meet this punk, maybe I can sell him some product. I meet him, he starts buying from me — thinks he's getting a better deal with me, which he's not — Anyway, I always meet him in this back room office on the ground floor which has an outside entrance. So I hang there, do a deal, watch some Knicks wit' him; I notice they got a *safe.* So I start coolin' with the kid on the regular, know what I'm sayin, and he's at work, but all his job requires is for him to hang in this office. I'm curious. So I befriend the motherfucker and within a week — he's kickin' it all to me! ... Turns out the club is selling mad drugs; yo, hallucinogens, speed, X — they're raking it in. And all the drug money goes in this base-

31

ment safe. Someone comes to pick it up every couple of days. They send the money to, like, Sweden, or some shit. The rest, they roll over to get more product. But here's the thing. They're an independent operation! They ain't paying no one off: no Mafia, no cops no gangs, no no-one! Nobody know shit about it! I mean, it's gonna be all over for them in a couple of weeks. But meantime, they got *money* down there. 750,000 dollars. Someone's coming to pick it up at midnight, which means we got three hours to get there first. Once we've stolen it, no one will care. We're not stealing from cops or mob — there's no reason for them to know or care what we do. And the disco can't say *shit* to anyone because they'll be slaughtered if any of the heavy hitters ever know how much cash they baggin' without paying off. This is a gift from *God,* yo!

EVERYTHING WILL BE DIFFERENT

BY MARK SCHULTZ

FREDDIE — Teenager.

SYNOPSIS: Teenage Charlotte's beautiful mother is dead, and in the midst of her own grief and her father's unwillingness to cope, she turns for comfort to the story of Helen of Troy, convinced that beauty, desire and fame can help her bring her mother back and punish the world that took her away in the first place. Getting beauty tips from her popular friend, seeking career advice on how to be a porn star from a guidance counselor who may or may not be having an affair with her, and searching for love from Freddie, the football jock who barely even knows she exists, Charlotte finds herself searching in fantasy for what she cannot find in reality.

TIME: The present.

(Warm, beautiful light. Charlotte's bedroom. Freddie enters. Bare-chested. Football in hand. He's beautiful.)

FREDDIE. Um. Hi. Charlotte. Um. Okay I know this is awkward and everything. Me just coming here and all. Like this. I mean I know I just really met you and everything. But I've seen you. Really. And I just gotta. I had to come and tell you. You know. And. This is embarrassing, I know. And I don't mean it to be. It's not supposed to be. I mean. But. Jesus, it's cold out, right? Anyway there's like a million things I wanna tell you right now, Charlotte. And I just. I don't know. Like. You have such a cool room. I really like your bedspread. Um. This is usually the other way around. Okay I've seen you. And. You are so. Pretty. I think. I mean. I think you're pretty. Right. Um. So I'll just come out and say it. Okay. I think I love you. Charlotte. I really do. And. It's not like this happens every day. You know. For me. I don't just like fall in love with people. It's hard. And I've really fallen for you. And I know it's stupid and like. Stupid and everything. But. I wanna know if maybe we can go out and be like boyfriend girlfriend or something I don't know. 'Cause I'm really. I'm. In love. With you. And it's hard. Keeping it inside. All the time. And I came here to say that. And ask you. You know. If we can maybe. Go out sometime. And. Eat something. Or. Watch a movie. Or I don't know. I got a great entertainment system at home. I could show you. DVD. Surround sound and everything. It's really cool. But. You know. We could go out and. Maybe I could touch you. And. Maybe you'd let me kiss you. I mean if that's okay. Is that okay? 'Cause I really love you. I really wanna be with you. It's so important to me right now. I really. Just had to come and tell you. I couldn't wait. Um. Shit I gotta get back to practice. Um. Okay. I love you. Please love me. Oh. And. I'm really sorry. About your mom. Being dead and all. That sucks. I gotta go.

EXPECTING ISABEL

BY LISA LOOMER

NICK — 40, Italian American, an artist and a believer.

SYNOPSIS: EXPECTING ISABEL is a comedy about the adventures of a New York couple trying to have a baby — by any means necessary. Their difficulties in conceiving lead them on an Alice in Wonderland-esque odyssey through the booming baby business as they negotiate the fertility trade, the adoption industry, and their own families.

(Nick is alone onstage.)

NICK. *(To audience.)* Okay, I'm gonna pick up the story and help her out. But first, you gotta understand something. I don't like to yell at my wife in the middle of Columbus Avenue — who does that? I was taught to turn the other cheek! Besides, you talked back, some nun'd pull your sideburns. And let me tell you something else. Until I met that hamster — I was a pretty happy guy! *(Glances offstage.)* Unlike some people ... Sure I saw some bad things go down when I was a kid — who didn't? I saw Nino Gallata push his brother off a balcony when they were moving furniture. Palmer Di Fonzo — I cut off his eyebrow accidentally with a pen knife — his mother came after me with a gun. Hercules Sorgini, smallest kid on the block, broke his neck in a sled accident, it was like this — *(Leans head on right shoulder.)* For a year they called him, "Ten After Six." And Wee Wee Scomo had a heart attack right on the dance floor in junior high. Doing the Twist. He jumped up, did some splits, never got up again. Best dancer at Holy Savior. What are you gonna do? You gonna tell a kid, "Wee Wee — don't dance"? Besides — *(Glances offstage.)* If his mother had worried about violent television and the crap they put in the school lunches — would it have saved him from the Twist!? *(Yells offstage.)* THAT'S WHY I DON'T WORRY! *(To audience.)* And that's why I've always been a happy guy. Like when I go to the bank. I don't think, "Oh shit — *(A la Miranda.)* "What if the guy on the other side of the cash machine's got a drug problem?" I don't even cup my hand over the keypad when I punch in my pin, which happens to be "Jude" by the way, after the patron saint of lost causes — and not on my worst days — not even on the day my wife left me on Columbus Avenue would I have had a problem telling you that — 'cause, hey, if you wanted to go out later, and use my favorite saint's name to steal my money — *(Yells offstage.)* I JUST WASN'T GONNA WORRY ABOUT IT! Besides … *(Pause; remembers.)* I didn't have any money. I spent my last fifty bucks on paint for the baby's room. And then we sold the apartment. Pretty fast too, because the couple who bought it were expecting a baby any day. Then me and Miranda had that fight in front of this Starbucks they put up where my favorite used art book store used to be … Then she went down to the sperm bank … *(Distraught.)* I did what any guy'd do — *(Pause.)* I went home to my mother.

FIVE KINDS OF SILENCE

BY SHELAGH STEPHENSON

BILLY — 50s.

SYNOPSIS: Billy controls his wife and two adult daughters to the extent that they can't leave the room without asking permission. He runs his family as a personal fiefdom, and the women are there to service him and his madness. He is violent, disturbed and sexually controlling. But he is also tragic, sad, a lost soul. One day his family shoots him dead. The play shows us a distorted world of madness, control and despair through the eyes of dead Billy and those of his family, struggling to understand reality outside their stifling tomb.

BILLY. One night, I dreamt I was a dog. The moon was out, I could smell it. Ice-white metal smell. I could smell the paving stones, wet, sharp. The tarmac road made my dog teeth tingle, it was aniseed, rubber, and then the lampposts, studded with smells they were. Studded with jewels of wood metal meat. And the stars pierced my dog nose like silver wires. A woman came out of her house, sickly the smell of her, rotten, she smelt of armpits and babies and fish and a hundred other things screaming at me like a brass band. I knew what she'd had for her tea. I knew she was pregnant. I could smell it. She didn't look at me, just walked straight on by, thought I was just a dog. I laughed a quiet dog laugh: you think I'm a dog but I'm Billy, I'm me. The night smells of soot and frost and petrol and beer. I'm at my own door now. I don't need to see it, it comes to meet me, a cacophony, the smells are dancing towards me, the smells of home. I'm inside the house now. Hot citrus smell of electric light. My wife, my daughters, stand up as I come into the room. Oh, home, the smells I love, all the tiny shimmering background smells, and the two I love the most, the two smells that fill the room like a siren. One of them is fear: burning tyres, vinegar, piss. And the other one, is the smell of blood, matted in Mary's hair. I gave her a good kicking before I went out.

FLESH AND BLOOD

BY PETER GAITENS

Adapted from the novel by Michael Cunningham

BILLY — Calls himself Will, adult son of Constantine.

SYNOPSIS: FLESH AND BLOOD, adapted from Pulitzer Prize–winning novelist Michael Cunningham's saga of twentieth-century American life, traces nearly 100 years in the lives of one archetypal family. Dominated by their volatile father, the Greek immigrant Constantine, and alienated from their mother, the genteel and ambitious Mary, the Stassos children, Susan, Billy and Zoe, struggle to build lives and find love in a culture undergoing tectonic shifts. Like lonely planets whose long, elliptical orbits collide in unexpected, sometimes violent ways, the members of the Stassos family, career both towards and away from one another in poignant, heartbreaking and sometimes shattering fashion.

WILL. Okay. Well, sort of okay. I had a real shit of a day.
[ZOE. I'm sorry.]
WILL. Oh, it's nothing. It's this kid in my homeroom class, your basic fuck-up. I've started keeping him after school, not just as punishment, but to go over the work with him in private so that maybe he learns a little something. I don't get paid for this, right? Well, today I get his parents to come in and I talk about how they could help encourage him at home, and they are nightmares. The mother's this tight-lipped little thing, like prim and trashy at the same time. And the father. Big fat guy, silent and mean-looking, and about halfway through the conversation he looks at me with this sly, patronizing gleam in his eyes and says, "You don't see a lot of men teachers." It's the first thing he's said. And glances over at his wife in this knowing way and she glances back. I mean, I may be the one chance this kid's got, and these assholes are going to turn him against me, that's what's clear, right? And it feels so fucking hopeless, you know? It's like there's this bottomless meanness and stupidity and it's so embedded and, I don't know, it seems to be *increasing,* it's like people are getting meaner and stupider and more and more proud of it.

38

FOOD FOR FISH

BY ADAM SZYMKOWICZ

BOBBIE — A young writer.

SYNOPSIS: Bobbie drops the pages from his novel into the Hudson River. They tell the story of three sisters: Sylvia, a reporter; Barbara, an agoraphobe (played by a man in drag); and Alice, a scientist with a plan to isolate and eliminate the gene for love. The three sisters are going to have to bury their father — when they get around to it.

(Bobbie, in his apartment, takes a letter out of an envelope. He reads it.)

BOBBIE. What? You fucker! You worthless fucker! *(Bobbie paces, he looks at the letter again. He crumples it up and throws it. He pounds the desk in anger, then puts a new sheet of paper in the typewriter. He types.)* Dear Sir, did you even read my masterpiece? If you had, you would not be sending me this form letter of rejection. Not unless you are indeed a complete and worthless moron. I do not accept you as an arbiter of real talent. I have more talent than all of you put together if it comes to that! You with your hackneyed conventions, have usurped the foremost places in art and consider nothing genuine and legitimate except what you yourselves do. Everything else you stifle and suppress. I do not accept you. I do not. It was optimistic of me to think that you were not an undiscerning fool.

Are you all conspiring against me, you with your form letters on separate letterheads that converge into one voice? As punishment for this, your highest crime, know that you have pushed me to eschew publication altogether. Know that you and the others and the world at large will miss out on the rest of my work which I shall never again let you touch with your dirty and destructive hands. My work belongs to eternity now. To the universe of ephemera. But never to you. May you find your just punishment knowing you have kept another genius from the hungry world who aches to hear him. Sincerely, The Author Who Would Have Made You Famous.

FROZEN

BY BRYONY LAVERY

RALPH — 30s, a murderer.

SYNOPSIS: One evening ten-year-old Rhona goes missing. Her mother, Nancy, retreats into a state of frozen hope. Agnetha, an American academic, comes to England to research a thesis: "Serial Killing — A Forgivable Act?" Then there's Ralph, a loner who's looking for some distraction. Drawn together by horrific circumstances, these three embark on a long, dark journey which finally curves upward into the light. Angry, humane and compassionate, FROZEN is an extraordinary play that entwines the lives of a murderer, the mother of one of his victims and his psychologist to explore our capacity for forgiveness, remorse and change after an act that would seem to rule them out entirely.

PLACE: England.

TIME: The present.

(Ralph, in his room, washing his hands at a sink.)

RALPH. You know
it's one of those days
you're just going to do it
you might do it
I suppose mostly I'm a bit of a cold fish
(He dries his hands carefully on a small, clean towel.)
but then, these times
things hot up
It's been a bit of a bad patch for me …
fucking landlady …
pardon my French …
despite I told her I don't eat lamb
despite I told her I'm not a big eater …
despite I made that clear …
turns up on the plate

and I've eaten it before I've said
"this isn't lamb is it…?"
and it *was* …
(Takes a small bottle of hand lotion, pours a dollop on one palm, starts to rub it into both hands.)
and I've gone out with
hoojit … Raymond Quantock …
and that wassname from work … Dick Bottle …
and I've kept up with them putting it away …
otherwise …
and drunk five lagers
and two …
(Counts in his head.)
… four …
Jack Daniels
and I've gone over on that damn foot again …
lightning strike of pain …
and it's put me in a strop
nobody better mess me with
nobody better
been like … offish
and …
(He's on a street somewhere.)
I just see her
and decide
I'm going to get her in the van
I just want to keep her for a bit
Spend some time with her.
I just do it.
It's a rush of blood.
Hello.
Hello.
I said "Hello"
are you deaf?
It's rude to ignore people.
are you loony?
you're loony.
I'm only being polite.
No need to get the hump.
Not with me.

I just said "Hello."
Hello.
Hello.
Hello.
I'm saying "hello" to you.
Least you can do is make conversation.
Kind of world is this
folk can't be sociable?
Polite.
Least you can do is make a response.
It's Bad Manners if you don't.
Bad manners.
Rude.
I said "Hello"
Hello
Hello
Hello
Hello
Hello then ...
finally ...
finally ...
she goes
"Hello"
I think she quite liked me
oh yes
She was interested

THE GIFTED PROGRAM

BY RUBEN CARBAJAL

STEVE MARONA — 18. New kid. Hyperactive body, but mind fogged in a haze of marijuana. Lives somewhat out of time and space; a kid who has been tossed around too much.

SYNOPSIS: In 1986, at the very bottom of Washington High's social food chain are the last remaining members of the Dungeons & Dragons club: four maladapted refugees from a defunct program for gifted and talented students who have been thrown into the harsh arena of an inner-city public high school. When the identity of a secret admirer is revealed, the school's rigid hierarchy is upended; for Washington High's four most unpopular students, the simple pursuit of an education becomes a fight for survival.

STEVE. *(Suddenly remorseful.)* I know, I know, I know. I'm sorry. *(Beat.)* Shit. *(Loudly, but to himself.)* No wonder I can't make friends. *(To the others.)* I'm sorry, I just don't have that buffer, you know, that everyone else has. I say what I think, just whatever pops in my head. I think its probably 'cause I'm stoned like, *ALL FUCKING DAY.* Damn, it's cold here. Do you know I've been to *eleven* schools in five years? I'm so fucking mixed up, honestly, I couldn't find this town on a fucking *map.*
[BILL. No kidding.]
STEVE. This is the most fucked up school I've ever been to. This town? Fucked *up.* It's so fucking harsh and boring and cold here. I can't *take* this place sober. At least I'm anonymous. People forget about me. I know my mom does, teachers do. They don't even know I'm *here* half the time. Makes skipping class much easier. The reason I move around so much is my dad is like hunting down my mom. He's violent. He always seems to find us. I think my mom thinks this place will be too miserable for even him. I'm tired of trying to fit in. I miss California. That was the best place. We'd cut class, bring a boombox and a bong to the beach, hang out, make a bonfire. Watch the sun go down. Make out, swim. I'll bet you guys never did anything like *close* to that in your entire fucking lives,

43

right? *(Beat.)* I'm sorry. *(Beat.)* That's sad. *(Beat, frustrated with himself.)* Man. *Big Mouth.* *(Beat.)* It's so fucking cold, I can't seem to get warm, *like EVER.* I crank up the heat in the house, but it's still *there,* you know? *In the bones.*

I AM MY OWN WIFE

BY DOUG WRIGHT

CHARLOTTE VON MAHLSDORF — 60s.

SYNOPSIS: Based on a true story, and inspired by interviews conducted by the playwright over several years, I AM MY OWN WIFE tells the fascinating tale of Charlotte von Mahlsdorf, a real-life German transvestite who managed to survive both the Nazi onslaught and the repressive East German Communist regime.

(The French doors at the rear of the room open, and — standing before us — Charlotte von Mahlsdorf. She is, in fact, a man, roughly sixty-five years old. Charlotte wears a simple black house dress with peasant stitching, a kerchief on her head, and an elegant strand of pearls. She gazes at the audience for a moment; the tiniest flicker of a smile dances on her lips. Then — surprisingly — she closes the doors as quickly as she appeared and is gone. A pause. The stage is empty again. In a moment, the doors reopen. Charlotte reappears. Cradled in her arms is a huge antique Edison phonograph complete with an enormous horn in the shape of a flower. She grins, satisfied, and sets the phonograph on a small plinth. She steps back for a moment to admire the music machine. When she speaks, it's in broken English, but the cadences of her voice are delicate; there's a musical lilt to her inflection. She has a German accent.)

CHARLOTTE. Thomas Alva Edison was the inventor of the first talking machine of the world in July of 1877. And you see, the record is not *ein plattenspieler; nein*. It is a cylinder, made of wax. And this record is working with 160 revolutions per minute, and is playing four minutes long. And the record is made by the National Phonograph company in Orange, New Jersey. At one time, I had over *fünfzehntausend* cylinders. *(Charlotte indicates a painting of the Edison phonograph with an attendant dog, its ears cocked to listen:)* And you see — on the wall — a painting: the dog, Nipper, "His Master's Voice." The most famous trademark in all the world. Next month, this phonograph will be half a century old. *(She begins to turn the handle on the phonograph, readying it for play.)*

For fifty years, I've been turning its crank.

The loudness depends on a big or a small horn. Metal horns are better for bands and the voices of men, and the wooden horns, they are better for the strings and the voices of the female. *Die Sopranistin.* And Edison's phonograph has in the needle a little sapphire. *(She plucks a tiny, disposable needle from a drawer concealed in the phonograph. She holds it up to the light, and says emphatically:)* *Nicht diamant; nur Sapphir.* And when it grazes the record, it sounds so nice. *(She installs the needle on the arm, then delicately places the arm on the wax cylinder. The machine begins to play; an old German waltz, scratchy and exquisite.)* In the Second World War, when the airplanes flew over Mahlsdorf, and the bombs were coming down, I played British and American records. And I thought, "They can hear in the airplanes that I am playing Edison records." I thought — if they hear me — they will know I'm their friend.

THE IMAGINARY INVALID

BY MOLIÈRE, TRANSLATED AND ADAPTED
BY JAMES MAGRUDER

ARGAN — 40s/50s, the imaginary invalid.

SYNOPSIS: In Molière's outrageous satire of medicine and its practitioners, the wealthy Argan enjoys poor health. Laxatives, suppositories, bloodlettings, and second and third opinions from the leading quacks are the order of his day — and hell on his wily, back-talking servant Toinette. His daughter Angélique is in love with the impoverished Cléante, but Argan wants to marry her to a medical dunce who can assure his father-in-law of lifetime health care. Cléante disguises himself as a music teacher to gain access to his love, but Béline, Argan's mercenary second wife, threatens to expose them. A disguised Toinette, sage advice from his brother, and a faked death scene finally teach Argan where to place his trust, and the play ends with Argan's ceremonious, pig-Latin induction into the medical profession.

SETTING: A private chamber in the home of Argan. Paris.

(Argan sits in his chair and calculates his medical bills.)

ARGAN. Three and two make five, plus five is ten, and ten makes twenty. "Item: on the twenty-fourth, an insinuating preparatory anal injection to soften, moisten, and refresh Monsieur's bowels." What I like about my apothecary Monsieur Fleurant is that his bills are expressed with such refinement … "and refresh Monsieur's bowels … thirty sous." Well Fleurant, it's one thing to be refined, it's another to gouge the sick. Thirty sous for an enema! Much obliged, but not that much; he charged me twenty for all the others; and, taking standard druggist's markup, twenty really means ten. There you are, ten sous. "Item: on the same day, a humour-purging double-strength suppository confected from rhubarb, rose-infused honey, etcetera, to sweep, irrigate, and reeducate Monsieur's lower intestine, thirty sous." I'll give you ten. "Item: that night, a soporific, narcotic, and hepatic julep compounded to induce sleep, thirty-five sous." No complaints there, it knocked me right out. So that's ten, fifteen, sixteen, seventeen and a half sous. "Item: the twenty-fifth, a laxative, made of fresh cassia and bay rhum, etcetera, according to Doctor Purgon's prescription, to evacuate Monsieur's bile, four francs." Purgon never told you to charge four francs. Let's do three. "Item: the twenty-sixth, a flatulatinacious injection to release Monsieur's ill winds, thirty sous." Ten sous for that, Fleurant. I almost burned a hole in the bedspread. "Item: the twenty-seventh, a strong medicine composed to hasten the production of number two — " ooh, such delicacy — "and to extradite the bad humours from Monsieur's body, three francs." Make it twenty, thirty sous. "Then a potion, made of twelve grains of ambergris, lemon and pomegranate syrup, etcetera, for rectal refreshment, five francs." Five francs? Jesus, Fleurant, at these prices, who can stay sick? You'll have to make do with four francs, twenty, forty sous. Sixty-three francs, four and a half sous. So, all totaled, this month makes one, two, three, four, five, six, seven, eight medications, and one, two, three, four, five, six, seven, eight enemas and four suppositories. Last month it was twelve medications, twelve enemas, and eight suppositories. *(Pause.)* I'm surprised I feel as well as I do. *(Calling out.)* You can take this away now. Is anybody here? I don't know why I waste my breath; it's hard to keep anybody on staff. *(He rings a little bell to summon the servants.)* No one can hear me; the bell is as weak as my constitution. Ding a ling a ling. Nothing. Ding a ling a ling. Are you all deaf or just pretending to be? Toinette! Ding a ling a ling! Toinette! Ding a ling a ling! That cow! Ding a ling a ling! I am not a well man! *(Starts really shouting.)* Ding a ling a ling! Filthy swine, you can all roast on a spit in hell! Have I been left here, a poor sick man, to languish by my lonesome? DING A LING A LING A LING A LING A LING A LING! My God, I've ruptured something. I have been left here to die! *(Death scene.)* Ding … a ling … a … ling.

LAST OF THE BOYS

BY STEVEN DIETZ

JEETER — Ben's friend, also a vet, 50s.

SYNOPSIS: Ben and Jeeter fought in Vietnam, and for thirty years they have remained united by a war that divided the nation. Joined by Jeeter's new girlfriend and her off-the-grid, whiskey-drinking mother, these friends gather at Ben's remote trailer for one final hurrah. As the night deepens, the past makes a return appearance, and its many ghosts come flickering to life. This is a fierce, funny, haunted play about a friendship that ends — and a war that does not.

PLACE: An abandoned trailer park, somewhere in the Great Central Valley of California.

TIME: The final summer of the twentieth century.

JEETER. Ben's done a lot of amazing things. *(Jeeter looks at Ben — waiting to see if he'll stop him. He gets only Ben's cold, hard stare.)* Has he told you about the three soldiers on a road? This was outside Dak To. *(To Ben.)* More of a path, really. Right? *(No response.)* Ben doesn't mind if I tell this. I'm his best friend in the world, *right?! (No response.)* Little red dirt path through the jungle. Three grunts on patrol. They come across a body. Viet Cong soldier. Seventeen, tops. Crispy-crittered by some napalm. But still alive. Some of his face gone. The soldiers spit on the ground. They all three know they gotta put this kid out of his misery. It's just a matter of who's gonna do it. The first soldier steps forward. "Fuck it" — he says — "I'll do it." Lifts his rifle to the kid's head — and then there's screaming. Someone running out of the jungle. An old woman. Hands in the air. Trying to stop them from doing this to — who? — her son, maybe? The soldiers are trying to shove her away — but this *mama-san* is wailing like a siren — and then she's *on top of her son.* Arms wrapped around him tight. And now the soldiers get it: She doesn't want him saved. She wants to *die with him.* Now, the second soldier steps forward — tries to pull the

49

woman off her son, but she's hangin' on for dear life — back and forth they roll — this sobbing mass rolling up and down the road — the second soldier is *screaming* at the old woman: *"DIDI MAU, DIDI MAU"* — trying to wrench them apart — and *crying* — now he's *crying* — the second soldier is shaking and crying *and he still can't pry this mother from her son.* The third soldier steps forward, cigarette in his mouth. He lifts his rifle. Aims it at the woman's leg. Fires. Her leg shatters. Aims at the other leg. Fires. She right away goes into shock — eyes rolling back in her head — still clutching her son. The third soldier turns to the others. "She wants to die with him. Let her die with him." And he walks on.

LOVE-LIES-BLEEDING

BY DON DeLILLO

SEAN — 35, son of ALEX, an artist.

SYNOPSIS: LOVE-LIES-BLEEDING focuses on the last years of a free-spirited artist, now left invalid after a second stroke. His estranged son, wife and ex-wife struggle over the ultimate question: How do they let him die with dignity? As DeLillo masterfully tackles the ethics of their decision, he amplifies what it truly means to be alive.

(Sean and the sitting figure of Alex, head raised, eyes open. Bottle of morphine one-quarter diminished.)

SEAN. I know it isn't true, what Lia says. She says that you can hear us. You can feel and think. You react, you're aware. I don't believe it. But even if I thought you could hear me, what would I say to you? I don't think I know what to say. I never did. I know what you would say if you could speak, if you chose to speak freely, in the spirit of little miracles. You would say, Not everything we feel has to be expressed, or can be expressed. We withhold some things. Some things are too powerful or too breakable. We withhold, we suppress, we whisper. We're free to do this, you would say. We whisper to our lovers. Why? Because some things are too precious to enter the world. Because too much can be said. Because love can't bear all this saying. But what about the son who sits in a room with his father? What happens then? I don't know. It was never clear to me who I was supposed to be in your presence. You were fixed forever within yourself. I was outside somewhere, watching us both. Not that I don't understand. I understand. Being a father had nothing to do with you. Having a child. It was an encroachment of the worst sort. It violated your seclusion, your private turmoil. It made you visible to yourself. I was proud of you. Did you know that? Proud to be the son of an artist. The cold-blooded bastard is a painter in a studio. One day, I'm twelve years old, standing in a corner to watch you work. Acrylic on Masonite. Hearing those fantastic words. Painting made sense to me, abstract painting made sense to me. It was acrylic on Masonite. And

51

cold black coffee in a paper cup. I drank some of your coffee and nearly fell down dead. *(Sean takes a seat near his father.)*

All right, here's a joke. It's a philosophical joke. I told it to my seniors in geophysics. Goes like this. Two tiny young fish are swimming in the sea. They come upon an older fish. He says to them, Hey, fellas, how's the water? The two young fish swim on past. They swim for many miles. Finally one fish says to the other, What the fuck is water? *(Sean studies his father.)*

It's a philosophical joke. What the fuck is water? *(Pause.)* In time I knew what I wanted. I wanted to look a certain way and sound a certain way. I worked at things. I trained myself to think a certain way. We were scared, weren't we, both of us.

MATCH

BY STEPHEN BELBER

TOBI — An older dancer and choreographer.

SYNOPSIS: Mike and Lisa Davis arrive at the apartment of Tobi Powell, who lives alone in Inwood, on the northern tip of Manhattan. They are there to interview him about his life as a dancer and choreographer, but it is soon evident that their agenda is as multilayered as the life story that Tobi begins to tell them. What happens next will either ruin or inspire them — and definitely change their lives forever.

PLACE: Upper Manhattan.

TIME: The present.

TOBI. *(Pause.)* It's funny about control, self-control. It's such a key ingredient in dance but it's something that you can't really teach. So what you do is try to get in there right at that point where the kids are still susceptible to discipline, with the hope that it can inspire them to *self*-control. It's actually what I love about teaching, that balance, or that *segue* where discipline becomes … inspiration. Where freedom is achieved through an imposed … *conformity.* *(Pause.)* Because you can set kids free by battening down the hatches so tight that they can't goddamn breathe. And if I was put on this earth for any reason, it was to do that; to set kids free. *(Pause.)* That's my thing. That's what I do, or try to do, and … and I'm sorry I didn't have the chance … I'm sorry I didn't have the chance to do that with *you.* For you. Mike. Michael. *(Pause.)* To set you free. *(Pause.)* I'm sorry. Because it's *my* loss.

53

THE MISER

BY MOLIÈRE, TRANSLATED AND ADAPTED BY JAMES MAGRUDER

HARPAGON — 40s/50s, father to Cléante and Elise.

SYNOPSIS: The widower Harpagon is so cheap he'd swipe the pennies off a dead man's eyes. His rebellious children, Cléante and Elise, are afraid to tell him of their romantic attachments: Cléante has fallen in love with the beautiful but penniless Mariane, and Elise is secretly engaged to Valère, a young charmer of unknown parentage who has flattered his way into being Harpagon's chief steward. When Harpagon reveals his own marital designs — he will wed Mariane himself and yoke Elise to the wealthy but aged Seigneur Anselme — children, suitors, disgruntled servants conspire to foil the miser. When Harpagon's treasure, buried in the backyard, is stolen, he rounds up all the suspects — including the audience — and threatens torture and imprisonment. Only the last-minute arrival of Seigneur Anselme, bearing secrets of his own, can unite the proper couples and restore Harpagon to his one true love — 40,000 pounds in gold.

HARPAGON.   Stop thief! Stop thief! Miscreant! Marauder! Assassin! I call upon the heavens for justice! My throat has been slit. Someone has stolen all my money! Where has she gone? Where is she hiding? Will I ever see her again? What will happen to her? Should I run? Should I stay? Stop thief! *(He catches himself by the arm.)* Give me back my money, you scoundrel! It's me. I'm losing my mind. Where am I? What am I? Who am I? I've lost my first, my last, my everything. Without her, I'm nothing. Why would you forsake me? I've always treated you so well. Did you find someone you like better? Do you wink and wiggle for him? Clank for him, run through his fingers, jingle in his pockets, tempt him with your sheen? Oh, inconstant fortune! You heartless, fickle jade, mistress of a thousand hands. No one could ever love you like I do. I can't live without you. I'm done for; I'm dying; I'm dead; I'm buried. Now I am but meal for worms, an unredeemèd carcass gone to dust. Only her return can bring me back to life. Will no one give her back? At least tell me who took her. What? What did you say? The criminal must have been spying on me for some time, choosing just the moment — when I was castigating my worthless son — to strike the mortal blow. Let us go and seek justice. I shall interrogate the entire house — servants, valets, sons, daughters, animals, and every last one of you *(Meaning the audience.)*. *(To the house manager and stage manager.)* Lock the doors. Turn up the houselights. Turn off the heat. No one gets out of here alive until I find the filthy crook. I'm not accusing anyone in particular. You all look guilty. *(He walks into the audience.)* But if I think you look suspicious, we'll have to do a cavity search. Ushers, get out your gloves, and woe betide he who is allergic to latex. What is he saying over there? Is he the thief? You were all watching the play — well, that one was asleep during the love scenes — so the thief has to be among you. Feel free to turn in your neighbor. It's an old French custom. What was that? Reward? Listen to her, she wants a reward. She thinks life is fair and people should get rewards for doing good deeds. People like you make me sick. Your reward, lady, is getting out of here with your honor intact. I don't know what you all think is so funny — my property was stolen! How would you like it if it happened to you? *(Pause.)* Alright, I'm counting to five — if no one fingers the thief, then I'm calling in the lawyers. We'll take down everybody's name and haul you to prison and I'll be happy to see you all hang.

MOBY-DUDE, OR: THE THREE-MINUTE WHALE

from THE OTHER WOMAN AND OTHER SHORT PIECES

BY DAVID IVES

Nathaniel — 17.

SYNOPSIS: In MOBY-DUDE, OR: THE THREE-MINUTE WHALE, Nathaniel, a stoned-out surfer dude, summarizes Melville's classic for his skeptical high-school teacher in a high-speed monologue.

NATHANIEL. *Call me Ishmael,* dude. Yes, Mrs. Podgorski, I *did* read *Moby-Dick* over the summer like I was supposed to. It was bodacious. Actually, y'know, it's "Moby-*hyphen*-Dick." The title's got this little hyphen before the "Dick." And what is the meaning of this dash before the "Dick"? *WHOAAA!* Another mystery in this awesome American masterpiece! A peerless allegorical saga of mortal courage, metaphysical ambiguity and maniacal obsession! *What,* Mrs. Podgorski? You don't believe I really *read* Herman Melville's *Moby-Dick, Or: The Whale?* Five hundred sixty-two pages, fourteen ounces, published in 1851, totally tanked its first weekend, re-released in the 1920s and recognized as one of the world's gnarliest works of Art? You think I copped all this like off the back of the tome, or by watching the crappy 1956 film starring Gregory Peck? Mrs. P., you been on my tail since middle school, do *I* get all testy? Do *I* say, what is the plot of *Moby-Dick* in under two minutes — besides a whale and a hyphen? *Moby-Dick* in two minutes, huh? Okay, kyool. Take out your stopwatch. Let's rip. *(A bell rings, as if to start a race. Very fast:)* Fade in. The boonies of Massachusetts, eighteen-hundred-and-something. Young dude possibly named Ishmael, like somebody in the Bible, meets-cute with, TAA-DAA!, *Queequeg,* a South Sea cannibal with a heart of gold. Maybe they're gay. Maybe they represent some east-west, pagan-Christian duality action. Anyway, the two newfound bros go to Mass and hear a sermon about Jonah — Biblical tie-in — then they ship out on Christmas Day (could be symbolical!) aboard *the U.S.S. Pequod* with its mysterious wacko Captain Ahab … *(Madman laughter.)* *Backstory!* Who is goofyfoot because the equally mysterious momboosaloid white sperm whale Moby-like-the-singer Dick bit Ahab's leg off. Freudian castration action. I mean this fish is big and spermaceous and his last name is "Dick," right? Moby is also a metaphor for God, Nature, Truth, obsessisical love, the world, the past, and white people. Check out Pip the Negro cabin boy who by a fluke — did I say "fluke" — goes wacko too. Ahab says, *"Bring me the head of the Great White Whale and you win this prize!"* Ka-ching! The crew is stoked, but *NOT* first-mate like-the-coffee-Starbuck. Ahab wants Moby, Starbuck wants whale juice. Could this be idealism versus capitalism? *Radical.* Queequeg tells the ship's carpenter to build him a coffin shaped like a canoe. *(Makes a spooky sci-fi sound.)* Foreshadowing! Then come lots of chapters everybody skips about the scientology of whales. Boring! Cut to Page 523, somewhere in the Pacific. *"Surf's up!"* Ahab sights the Dick. He's totally amped. The boards hit the waves, the crew chases the Dick for three whole days, bottom of the third Ahab is ten-toes-on-the-nose, he's aggro, Moby goes aerial, Ahab's in the zone, he fires his choicest harpoon, the rope does a three-sixty round Ahab's neck, Ahab crushes out, Moby totals the *Pequod,* everybody goes down except our faithful narrator Ishmael, who boogies to safety on Queequeg's coffin … *(Deeper voice:)* "AND I ONLY AM ESCAPED ALONE TO TELL THEE!" *(Normal voice:)* Roll final credits. The end! *(Bell rings.)* Did I leave anything out? Pretty, like, canonical, right? So what do you say, Mrs. Podgorski? Advance placement? *Tubular, babe!* You want go catch a cup of Starbucks…?

MONTHS ON END

BY CRAIG POSPISIL

BEN — Phoebe's fiancé, 30s.

SYNOPSIS: In a series of comic scenes we follow the intertwined worlds of a circle of friends and family whose lives are poised between happiness and heartbreak. The circle centers on Phoebe and Ben, who are engaged to be married but have some lingering doubts. Phoebe's wedding day meltdown isn't helped by her father, who, trying to calm her fears, tells her to "Pretend you're in an airplane that's crashing …" As the year draws to a close, a fight over The Beatles threatens to break up Ben and Phoebe, but a death bonds them more strongly together.

PLACE: A Los Angeles hotel room.

TIME: November, the present.

BEN. *(Reading from the pad and going from memory.)* Wade and I became friends when we were fifteen and met during our fourth period theater class in tenth grade. Over the next few months as we became best friends, I remember thinking I couldn't wait until we were thirty so I could say I'd known him for half my life. *(Slight pause.)* Well, I'm past thirty now, but I feel like I've known him all my life. And in a way, I think I have and always will, despite what the calendar may try to say. *(Slight pause.)*
Because I live in New York and he lived in Los Angeles, Wade and I could sometimes go months without talking or over a year without seeing each other. But we always picked up right where we left off, like we saw each other everyday. We could spontaneously break into scenes from *Monty Python and the Holy Grail.* Much to the dismay of those around us. Time and distance didn't seem to affect our relationship. *(Slight pause.)*
Which was good because Wade was always on the go … working … traveling. But that was Wade. He could never sit still for too long. I used to feel lazy next to him. He had such drive and energy, he was always moving from one project right into the next. And

58

when he learned he was HIV-positive, it was natural for him to become an activist and scholar where the disease was concerned, while still giving his all to his work at the museum. *(Pause.)*

It was very important to Phoebe and me that Wade was able to be a part of our wedding last summer. Wade never let an opportunity pass without telling me he thought she was terrific, and she felt the same about him. And the three of us always had a great time together, be it visiting the stark Joshua Tree National Park or going to Seventies disco night at the Apache Club, a gay bar in L.A., where both Wade and Phoebe were asked to dance, and I, unaccountably, was not. *(Pause.)*

I know there will always be things I want to share with Wade, but won't be able to now. Even in the past three days there have been things he would have gotten a kick out of. *(Slight pause.)* Not a half hour after he died, for instance. Phoebe and I were with him and his family in the hospital. It was a little after seven-thirty. After crying and hugging the others, Phoebe and I went out into the hall. A few minutes later Paige, Wade's sister, came out, leaving her parents alone with him. And the three of us are sitting there on the floor of the hospital corridor, still crying ... when at eight o'clock a voice comes over the P.A. system to announce ... "Visiting hours are now over." *(Slight pause.)* Which just seemed hysterical to me, and I'm trying not to laugh, but I see Phoebe giggling quietly and Paige smiling. Seeing each other we all burst out laughing. *(Pause.)*

Later that night back at the hotel, I dialed Wade's number to leave Paige a message, and I was so startled to hear his voice on the answering machine I couldn't remember why I called. Then Phoebe and I called back just so we could hear Wade one last time. *(Slight pause.)*

You know, when a person dies I think it's the sound of their voice we miss the most. The face is so often captured in a photograph, but the voice is a rare thing. And it's really the voice that defines a person, because it's through their voice we come to know their thoughts and feelings, everything about them. So to miss the sound of a voice is to miss the very being of that person. *(Pause.)*

We're gathered here because we were lucky enough to have had Wade in our lives. We were all touched by his intelligence, his humor, compassion and vitality. And despite the pain we now feel, how much poorer would our lives be if we couldn't think of him and say, "He was my son," or "He was my brother," or "He was my friend"?

THE MOONLIGHT ROOM

BY TRISTINE SKYLER

JOSHUA — 16 years old. Smart, restless, someone who is always trying to rise above the turmoil he feels.

SYNOPSIS: A dark tale of urban adolescence and family life, THE MOONLIGHT ROOM is set in the emergency room of a New York City hospital as two high-school students wait for news on the fate of a friend. As the situation worsens and family members begin to arrive, the play examines the idea of "at-risk" youth, and the potential for risk within your own family.

PLACE: The action takes place in the waiting area of the emergency room of a hospital, on the Upper East Side of Manhattan, in New York City.

TIME: The present.

JOSHUA. Remember Eben Macauley? He disappeared. Or was kidnapped. One or the other. No one ever saw him again. One day in the summer between fourth and fifth grade I was riding around. I saw him standing outside 158 on York Avenue. He was doing the summer program and he was waiting for his mom to come get him. He had just gotten a haircut and I remember his scalp was really pink. And he was squinting his eyes, cause people with blond hair and blue eyes can't see in bright sunlight. I waved at him from my bike, and I said, "Yo Eben, what's up?" But he didn't hear me. So I kept going and looped around the block and when I passed the corner again he was gone. That was the last time I saw him. And a week later he disappeared. His parents mobilized the entire city. I think the mayor started a task force. There were posters on every bus. His father quit his job. Their lives completely stopped. The only thing they lived for was to find their son. They lived in the Pavilion. That building on 77th with the pool on the roof? I'd hung out with him a little bit in the summers, when we were younger. I would have dinner at his house. It was weird, the way the whole family sat down together, every night, at the table … They had this room, it had white linoleum floors, and toys in there and books. It faced the East River and at night the moon reflected off the water and the whole family would go in there after dinner. They called it the moonlight room.

[*SAL. I remember him. I remember seeing the signs on the buses.*]

JOSHUA. *(Pause.)* You can't help but wonder. Wonder what it is to wonder. Not knowing where he is or if he'll ever come home. What that must be like to live with every day.

MR. CHARLES, CURRENTLY OF PALM BEACH

from THE NEW CENTURY

BY PAUL RUDNICK

MR. CHARLES.

SYNOPSIS: *Mr. Charles is the most joyously, fiercely, politically incorrect creature imaginable, who hosts his own late-night cable show in South Florida, taking questions from the audience. Mr. Charles, in his bold yellow slacks, espadrilles and provocatively vivid hairstyle, confronts every hot-button topic from gay marriage to the history of gay theater, finally delving into the highest matters of identity and flamboyance.*

PLACE: *A bare-bones public-access television studio in Florida.*

TIME: *Early evening.*

(Buoyant big-band theme music is heard, something very upbeat and welcoming. Mr. Charles enters. He is ageless. He is stylish, haughty and bold. He wears a fairly obvious, fairly blonde hairpiece, a tomato red blazer over a gingham shirt, with an Hermés scarf knotted Apache-style at his throat, colorful espadrilles, white, lemon or lime green slacks, and a necktie knotted as a belt. His face boasts a not particularly discreet coat of moisturizer, bronzer and a touch of mascara. His image is not transvestite but Palm Beach decorator or antiques dealer. He is glorious. After smiling and posing for the audience, Mr. Charles sits on the throne-like chair. He picks up a letter from the small table.)

MR. CHARLES. *(Reading from the letter.)* "What causes homosexuality?" *(He puts down the letter.)* I do. I am so deeply homosexual, that with just a glance, I can actually turn someone gay. *(He glances at someone in the audience.)* Well, that was easy. Sometimes, for a lark, I like to stroll through maternity wards, to upset new parents.

I am Mr. Charles, and I am currently residing here in Palm Beach, in semi-retirement. In exile. You see, I was asked to leave New York. There was a vote. Today's modern homosexuals find me an embarrassment. This is because, on certain occasions, I take what I call — a nelly break. For example: A few months ago, I attended an NYU conference, on gay role models. And this young man stood up and said, *(In an earnest, manly voice.)* "We must show the world that gay people are not just a pack of screaming queens, with eye makeup, effeminate hand gestures and high-pitched voices." And I just said ... *(He stands and does a nelly break, shrieking and mincing and flapping his wrists; he might burble, "Oh girl! Oh Miss Thing! Oh Mary!" Then he stops and sits, instantly calm again.)* It just happened. I went nelly. I just began babbling, in Gay English. You know, Shebonics. Oh, or another time, I was attending a rally. And a woman approached me and she said, "I would like you to donate five thousand dollars, to support our boycott of Hollywood films which portray homosexuals as socially irresponsible, promiscuous, and campy." *(Another delirious nelly break.)* And so, I was asked to leave the city. As revenge, I have begun to broadcast this program on cable channel 47, a show which I call, "Too Gay." It can be found at four A.M. on alternate Thursdays, in between "Adult Interludes" and "Stretching With Sylvia." Poor dear.

PIG FARM

BY GREG KOTIS

TEDDY — 40s or older, used to be an idealist, toughened by hard reality. He suspects mankind is no damn good.

SYNOPSIS: On a struggling pig farm somewhere in America, Tom and Tina (with the help of Tim, their hired hand) fight to hold on to everything they own — namely, a herd of 15,000 restless pigs. Dumping sludge into the river has driven Tom to drink, and Tim seems to have caught Tina's eye, but when Teddy, a gun-toting officer of the Environmental Protection Agency arrives to inspect the operation, life on the farm explodes, implodes, then explodes again.

TEDDY. Got to say, Tom, quite a sight. All them pigs rushing down the driveway, rushing to freedom. Trevor and Tyler screeching the van into place just before the herd crossed the property line, then the PANG! PANG! as each pig smashed into the van. Thousands of pigs, ramming that van into nothing more than a crumpled up ball of aluminum foil. Trevor and Tyler got squished a bit, but they've got war stories now. A feed meal show is one thing. A pig run? Well, that's another thing altogether. You see, most jobs for us consist of counting herds of pigs and comparing the tallies we get to the tallies you present in your voucher. But today we were inside with the pigs, feeling them brush about past our pant-legs, feeling the warmth of their bodies as they made their way through the muck. And when they bolted? Why, it was nothing less than a blizzard of little tan hooves and rolling, jolting pig bellies. What was the name of the sow I caught?
[TINA. Ol' Bess.]
TEDDY. Ol' Bess. Gave me a run for the money, though, didn't she? Big old girl, heaving and screeching. Something about the look in her eye after I tackled her said she knew more than we'd ever given a pig credit for. Good Ol' Bess. Close, close by yards, but still a few yards from the brush line.
[TOM. It was a good catch, Teddy.]
TEDDY. There are those who say city folks haven't the slightest

idea where food comes from, or how the hell it gets to the table. There are those who say city folks haven't the slightest notion what it takes to fill a nation's belly full of meat. Well, I have a notion. Now I do. It all makes a man want to work a farm, Tom. Makes a man understand what it is you're fighting for, here.

POLISH JOKE

BY DAVID IVES

JASIU — 30ish.

SYNOPSIS: A comedy about ethnic identity and the eternal American search for "roots." Jasiu is a Polish American who has been taught not to value his own roots, so he decides to make his own roots, reinventing himself first as a sort of nonethnic everyman, then as an "Irishman." Jasiu's adventures take him through a job interview with an Ur-WASP; an attempt to become a Catholic priest; to a doomed love affair with a Jewish woman; to a wacky Irish travel agency where he has to prove that he is Irish before he can buy a ticket; and to a doctor more interested in ethnic pain than in healing. Jasiu is also bedeviled by a reappearing Polish relative and the ghost of a dead Polish patriot. In the end, by trying to get away from his ethnic background, Jasiu finds out who he is and what it means to be "a Pole."

PLACE: America and elsewhere.

TIME: Now and then.

JASIU. I once had a curious dream. I dreamt that I was born into a Polish settlement in a large American city, and my dream name was Jan Bogdan Sadlowski. And in my dream I had Polish parents and went to a Polish school where we sang Polish songs. And all these things seemed completely normal to me — maybe because everybody around me was having the same dream I was. Or maybe because my dream was indistinguishable from real life. And at the heart of the heart of my dream there was a terrible hunger and a dissatisfaction, as if I was running from something. And I knew what I was running from but not what I was looking for. And then in my dream I ran into a wonderful girl named Rachel who for some reason loved me … I was on my way to see her, but I was in the wrong part of town. I was in a flower shop but I couldn't buy any flowers. And I had a bus to catch, so I ran out into the street, where the lights of my bus were shining in the distance. *(Lights change to a spotlight on Jasiu.)* I started to chase it. The night was dark all around me but I kept running. And I ran and I ran and I cried out, *Wait! Wait! That's my bus!* And as the headlights of the approaching bus burned into the back of my brain, two things hit me right between the eyes. First, an amazing revelation, the answer to all my problems. Second — the bus.

PRAYING FOR RAIN

BY ROBERT LEWIS VAUGHAN

JIM — 19/20ish.

SYNOPSIS: Marc, a high school jock suddenly stripped of his identity after a near-crippling motorcycle accident, has been adrift since the crash. His spiraling journey into self-destruction leads him into a lengthy detention with Miss K, a generous but firmly principled teacher. Although Miss K is able to make inroads with Marc, he continues his downward descent. Despite his resistance, his old friends, Jim and Chris, exert a powerful pull on him, yielding in the end staggeringly tragic results.

PLACE: The entire play takes place on The Bluffs at Dragon's Tongue, which is a red sandstone rock formation.

TIME: The past as Marc thinks about it and the present as he sees it.

JIM. You know, I was jealous of you. Yeah. I don't think I ever let it show, but I was. Fuckin' — you — man. You know what really gets me? You go off and be Mr. Football and leave me sittin' with shit-for-brains Chris, and you really don't even change. I couldn't hate you even though I was jealous 'cause you didn't change. You treated us the same as you always did. Mystery Marc. You know what's funny? If I was you, I wouldn't have done what you did. I wouldn't 'a stood around — I'd 'a been fuckin' outta here, kid. Gone. That's part of the reason I just wait. Look at me. Look at me you fuckin' — *(Marc doesn't turn. Jim busts down to Marc and grabs his face and forces their eyes to meet.)* I just wait because I know you better than you know yourself. I know you'll be back. You are such a natural-born fuck-up, kid, shit. You do your little make-up lesson and you pass and then you're right back where you started and guess what? In three weeks we're going to the bluffs and somebody's gonna die …

PYRETOWN

BY JOHN BELLUSO

HARRY — A handsome, clever young man in a wheelchair.

SYNOPSIS: Louise is a divorced mother of three, getting by on welfare checks and child support in a depressed, industrial New England town. Harry has been in a wheelchair since a childhood accident. Their paths cross in an emergency room as Louise seeks out care for her daughter's mysterious sickness. Yearning for connection beyond his online friends and his pile of Russian novels, Harry reaches out to help Louise navigate her daughter's care. More compatriots than lovers, they find solace with each other for a brief and intense interlude before their paths diverge.

PLACE: A New England town.

TIME: The present.

HARRY. I grew up near the marina, did I tell you that? I'd always go out and throw rocks at the boats, I love throwing rocks at the boats, all those expensive yachts, I pick up rocks in the middle of the night and throw them at the yachts. And as I grew up, the stronger I got, the bigger the rocks that I'd throw.

But the thing I always used to do, I would stand on the rocks, standing up straight, and I'd step down into the dirt and I'd dig my feet and toes deep into the soil, like a wild beast. *(Louise stares out the window, smoking her cigarette, quietly listening. Harry stares ahead.)* And with my feet in the soil, I would feel the earthworms, tickling my toes, crawling under my feet, squirming around, and it felt so strange, y'know? But it also felt, natural, like I was part of nature and I loved those moments. With my toes in the soil, I was a king 'cause I was connected to nature, and to dirt and rocks and worms and no one else in the world was connected the way I was, and that was magnificent.

But then my diving accident happened and I was in the hospital for a really long time and they had to teach me all kinds of things

69

that I thought I already knew, like how to button my shirt and pick up a fork and lots of other things but there really was only one thing on my mind and that was the thought that kept repeating in my head over and over:

"If I can't stand up, and walk on those rocks, and tip those rocks over and shove my feet into the soil and feel those earthworms tickling my feet, then what does that say about me? Where does that leave me? How do I fit into this thing called 'nature' now?" *(He looks to her, speaking to her. She continues looking out the window.)* But it sounds strange to say, and this answer has only come to me in the last few years, since my mother died, but when I see a beautiful woman like you, Louise, it's then that I remember, that I still feel desire, still, even now. That's how I can still fit into nature, because I still feel desire, I still want to kiss a woman like you, and touch her breasts, and feel the way that the shape of her breasts change when I touch them with my fingers, I want to put my mouth close to there and I want to feel alive. I don't want to push people away from me anymore. I don't want to fly around in circles. I want to feel close to people; desire. That's how I fit into nature. I never feel cracked or broken, when I feel desire. Those are the moments, when I feel fine.

RABBIT HOLE

BY DAVID LINDSAY-ABAIRE

JASON — A 17-year-old boy.

SYNOPSIS: Becca and Howie Corbett have everything a family could want, until a life-shattering accident turns their world upside down and leaves the couple drifting perilously apart. RABBIT HOLE charts their bittersweet search for comfort in the darkest of places and for a path that will lead them back into the light of day.

PLACE: Larchmont, New York.

TIME: The present.

JASON. Dear Mr. and Mrs. Corbett, I wanted to send you my condolences on the death of your son, Danny. I know it's been eight months since the accident, but I'm sure it's probably still hard for you to be reminded of that day. I think about what happened a lot, as I'm sure you do, too. I've been having some troubles at home, and at school, and a couple people here thought it might be a good idea to write to you. I'm sorry if this letter upsets you. That's obviously not my intention. Even though I never knew Danny, I did read that article in the town paper, and was happy to learn a little bit about him. He sounds like he was a great kid. I'm sure you miss him a lot, as you said in the article. I especially liked the part where Mr. Corbett talked about Danny's robots, because when I was his age I was a big fan of robots, too. In fact I still am, in some ways — ha ha. I've enclosed a short story that's going to be printed in my high school lit magazine. I don't know if you like science fiction or not, but I've enclosed it anyway. I was hoping to dedicate the story to Danny's memory. There aren't any robots in this one, but I think it would be the kind of story he'd like if he were my age. Would it bother you if I dedicated the story? If so, please let me know. The printer deadline for the magazine is March 31st. If you tell me before then, I can have them take it off. *(Becca flips through the story enclosed.)* I know this probably doesn't make things any better, but I wanted you to know how terrible I feel about Danny. I know that no matter how hard this has been on me, I can never understand the depth of your loss. My mom has only told me that about a hundred times — ha ha. I of course wanted to say how sorry I am that things happened the way they did, and that I wish I had driven down a different block that day. I'm sure you do, too. Anyway, that's it for now. If you'd like to let me know about the dedication, you can email me at the address above. If I don't hear from you, I'll assume it's okay. Sincerely, Jason Willette. *(Beat.)* P.S. Would it be possible to meet you in person at some point?

RAG AND BONE

BY NOAH HAIDLE

T-BONE — A big pimp whose heart feels too damn much.

SYNOPSIS: Two brothers, Jeff and George, run The Ladder Store, which is actually a front for their business in black-market hearts. In the world of RAG AND BONE, hearts are bought and sold for people who can't feel enough. The play begins when George steals the heart of a poet. The play then follows the poet with no heart; a hooker with a heart of gold; T-Bone, her pimp who feels too damn much; and the Millionaire, who eventually receives the poet's heart and sees a whole different world. Jeff and George recently lost their mother, but they put her heart into George's body, and all of a sudden he's wearing a dress, drinking martinis and cooking pot roasts. This is a heartfelt (excuse the pun) comedy about the limits of feeling, and the consequences of either feeling nothing or too damn much.

PLACE: Various locations in a place that gets less oxygen and sunlight than the rest of the world.

TIME: Right now.

(On the street. T-Bone.)

T-BONE. What's up, [place of performance]?! Goddamn cold out tonight, huh? My name's T-Bone. I'm a pimp. And let me tell you it was not my first choice of jobs. No sir. I was gonna be a pilot. First time I saw a plane I was seven years old. My grandma took me to the airport. We ate bologna sandwiches in the parking lot and watched the planes taking off, talking about where they was going. This one's going to Tahiti. That one's going to New Orleans. This one's going to Bermuda. We talked about all the people on them planes. How happy they was to be going somewhere else. Ever since then I wanted to be a pilot. Instead I became a pimp. I think about all the places I woulda seen if I had been a pilot. All the clouds. All the oceans. When my grandma died I spread her ashes at the airport, hoping maybe they would get somewhere good on one of them planes. Tahiti. New Orleans. Bermuda. I never been on a plane but I'm saving up. Pretty soon I'm gonna get on a plane and never come back. Not ever. Even in my dreams I won't come back.

THE REST OF THE NIGHT

BY ROBERT LEWIS VAUGHAN

KEITH — 30s to 40s, a deputy.

SYNOPSIS: *Miller and Malia Hunter have a troubled marriage, but they get by just fine until Miller slips into a pattern of destructive drinking. Life is hard enough in the Texas panhandle, but Miller's downward spiral begins to unravel the Hunter family and seriously threaten their son Eric's upbringing. After a bout with the bottle, Miller is hauled into jail and the new deputy, Keith, is dispatched to inform Malia that she must come into town and collect her husband. Malia and Keith see sparks the moment they lay eyes on one another. Keith's entrance into the Hunters' lives only complicates things further as young Eric strikes up a friendship with the new deputy. Malia is soon torn apart and must choose between the two men. Will she fight to keep her family together, or will she accept Keith's offer to take care of her and Eric as they should be taken care of?*

PLACE: *The play takes place in the back yard of the Hunter home in the Texas Panhandle, sixty or so miles from Amarillo.*

TIME: *The distant past. The play spans ten or so years.*

KEITH. No. My wife was a partyer. Oh boy, she liked her good times. I liked mine too, but … She liked hers more. I had as much fun as she did when we'd go out dancin' and drinkin' and raisin' our hell. I'd drink my beers, she'd drink her whiskey sours and I'd eat her cherries. What the hell, I mean … we were nothin' but kids when we first got married and was doin' that. What else was there? It didn't seem like there was too many options for us, that we cared for anyway. So we kept on partyin' and pretendin' that we were fine … and, we knew we weren't. Then we started fightin'. I don't have a bad temper. I never did. I just don't have it in me, but she did. She was so hot-headed sometimes that I'd think there was somethin' wrong with her. So. We'd fight and we'd make up, and she'd wanna go play and I'd say no and we'd fight some more, and she'd go by herself and I'd sit home wonderin' what kind of man I was lettin' my wife go off like that.

[*MALIA. Keith —]*

KEITH. Things went on like that for a while, and then I got tired of sittin' home when she'd run off. I followed her and I wish I hadn't'a 'cause I didn't like what I found. I loved her to death, Malia, I really did. I couldn't think about any other women when I was with her. Not like that anyway. I thought I was about the luckiest guy in town, but ... People started tellin' me I better get a better grip if I was plannin' on keepin' her, so I tried. But we had two different things in mind, and all we started doin' was fightin' more than we ever did and she started cheatin' on me for real. And we had bigger fights — she used to throw things — boy, I tell you, she had one hell of a good arm. She run outside this last time and she was goin' — I mean she was leavin', and I run out after her and was hell-bent for leather gonna drag her butt back in the house. She was in the car and I run up and dove into the window and tried to get the keys and she's got the damn thing started. She's hittin' me and scratchin' me and bitin' me and ... she ... starts backin' up and I don't know what hits me but I slipped and fell ... she run right over my leg. (*Malia gasps, then laughs, partly because she can't believe her ears and partly because she doesn't know what else to do.*)

[*MALIA. I'm sorry. I'm so ... I don't mean to —]*

KEITH. Hell, I laugh about it now. What else can I do? It must'a looked funny. We had a couple neighbors waterin' their grass standin' around with their mouths plumb hangin' open, not knowin' what the hell to do with me layin' there in the driveway with my leg run over. She was drivin' off down the street callin' me every name in the book and hollerin' back that she hoped it hurt worse than it looked like it did.

THE RETREAT FROM MOSCOW

BY WILLIAM NICHOLSON

EDWARD — A schoolteacher in his late 50s.

SYNOPSIS: Edward and Alice have been married for thirty-three years. Their thirty-year old son, Jamie, visits them for the weekend to find that this is the Sunday his father has picked to leave Alice for another woman. Jamie watches helplessly as his parents' marriage crumbles, and his mother is overwhelmed with bewilderment and pain. This is a play without villains — both Edward and Alice are good people trying to do their best — but the damage done by Edward's departure is devastating. Jamie, caught in the middle, slowly realizes that he's not an impartial witness but one of the combatants. His struggle is to understand both his parents and, like them, to survive the emotional hurricane that has ripped through their lives.

PLACE: England.

TIME: The present.

EDWARD. She found me in the staff room. There was something I'd forgotten, or failed to do, something very minor. She went for me in front of my colleagues, which I consider unacceptable. What could I do? I walked out of the staff room. To avoid the embarrassment of it. She came after me, saying, "Talk to me. Answer me. Look at me." I walked faster and faster, not really thinking where I was going. She followed. "Talk to me. Answer me. Look at me." I went out onto the playing fields. She followed. "Turn and face me, you coward. You can't run forever." And of course, the playing fields don't go on forever. So I turned back, and there she was. I tried to walk past her, but she kept in my way, shouting at me. "Talk to me. Answer me. Look at me." Then she started to take off her clothes. She took off her jersey, and threw it at me. She was wearing a T-shirt underneath, like a teenager. She took that off, threw it at me. Then her skirt. Then her bra. It was unbearable. She looked pitiful, standing there, trembling, in the middle of the playing field. So of course I had to turn and face her. And she said, "There. I've made you look at me at last."

THE REVENGER'S TRAGEDY

BY JESSE BERGER

Freely adapted from the original text by THOMAS MIDDLETON, CYRIL TOURNEUR or ANONYMOUS — Incorporating material from the writings of FRANCIS BACON, JOHN DONNE, THOMAS KYD, JOHN MARSTON, WILLIAM SHAKESPEARE and JOHN WEBSTER

SPURIO — The Duke's bastard son. Edmund in *Lear*, although not as clever. Despite his protestations, he starts to like screwing the Duchess, and that distracts him from the job at hand.

SYNOPSIS: This mesmerizing Jacobean thriller, written a few years after Hamlet, *is a searing examination of humankind's social need for justice and our animal desire for vengeance. Vindice, the "Revenger," sets off a chain reaction of havoc in a corrupt and decadent Venice, which exposes outrageous indulgences and government hypocrisy, and ends in a coup de théâtre massacre of epic proportions. Part black comedy, part social satire, the play is a gleefully macabre plot-twisting blender full of Shakespeare's greatest hits.*

PLACE: The court of Venice.

SPURIO.
    How one incestuous kiss picks open hell.
    Duke, thou didst do me wrong and by thy act
    Adultery is my nature.
    Faith, if the truth were known, I was begot
    After some gluttonous dinner — some stirring dish
    Was my first father; when deep healths went round
    And ladies' cheeks were painted red with wine,
    Their tongues as short and nimble as their heels
    Uttering words sweet and thick, and when they rose
    Were merrily disposed to fall again.
    In such a whispering and withdrawing hour

Was I stolen softly — O damnation met
The sin of feasts, drunken adultery.
I was begot in impudent wine and lust;
I feel it swell me, my revenge is just.
Stepmother, I consent to thy desires,
I love thy mischief well. But I hate thee —
And those three curs thy sons, wishing confusion,
Death and disgrace may be their epitaphs.
As for my brother, the Duke's 'only son,'
(Enter Lussurioso.)
Whose birth is more beholding to report
Than mine, and yet perhaps as falsely sown,
I'll loose my days upon him; hate all I!
Duke, on thy brow I'll draw a bastard's smile:
A bastard should make cuckolds by his nature,
Sith he is the son of a cuckold-maker.

RIDICULOUS FRAUD

BY BETH HENLEY

KAP CLAY — The middle brother.

SYNOPSIS: A disastrous New Orleans wedding rehearsal dinner is the latest in a series of unfortunate events that befall the Clay brothers in this boisterous and bittersweet comedy. Daddy's in jail for fraud, Uncle Baites has taken up with a panhandler, and Lafcad's just called off his own wedding. What family doesn't have its ups and downs? Winner of the Pulitzer Prize for Crimes of the Heart, *Henley returns to her Southern roots with an equally outsized and even more achingly poignant saga of three grown brothers trying to outrun a family history that tends to the worst-case scenario.*

PLACE: Kap's cabin and backyard, deep in the woods. Winter.

TIME: Five years before Hurricane Katrina.

Kap's cabin, deep in the woods. The following winter. Late afternoon. Kap moves around the cabin eloquently practicing duck calls. He has been drinking scotch. Maude is at a butcher block, cleaning and gutting mallards. Her health has greatly improved. She has never looked more alive.

KAP. The three most important things you have to take on a duck hunt — I don't care whether it is saltwater, freshwater, swamp. You have to have a gun, you have to have some shells, some bullets to kill the duck. And after that the next thing I'd take would be this. *(He indicates duck call.)* Over waders, over decoys, over dogs, over anything. Because if you know how to use it right, many times you can bring that duck right to you with nothing else around. They're hearing the sound and they're looking for the ducks and even if they don't see them, they come to the sound. And you can bring 'em in range to kill them. After guns and shells that would be the next thing. Takes years to learn to do it right. You can learn how to sound like a duck pretty quickly, but then the next part is you're

81

actually talking to those birds. When they're coming in you pick a bird, you watch how that bird responds. Even if there're a hundred birds, I'm talking to that one bird. In those flocks there'll be some dominant bird that'll kind of control the flock. A lot of time it's a big ol' hen. She decides whether they're going to light or not light. I'm talking to that one bird. Convincing her to come to me. Basically it goes: demand, beg, plead. *(Kap blows on his duck call: demand, beg, plead.)* It's entirely an illusion.

ROULETTE

BY PAUL WEITZ

JON — 40s.

SYNOPSIS: Dysfunction and black comedy reign in suburbia when Jon, an affable businessman and father, descends to his kitchen one morning takes a revolver from his briefcase, loads one bullet, spins the cylinder, places it against his temple and pulls the trigger. Nothing. Jon tidies up and leaves for work. His troubles, however, follow him there. Jon's wife, Enid, is cuckolding him with his best friend, Steve, who shows up suddenly at Jon's office to ask for a loan. Back at home, Jon's daughter Jenny, is planning on sleeping over at her boyfriend's house and attempting to enlist her mother to convince Jon it's all right. Trying to come to grips with this rapidly breaking home is Jon's perpetually anxious son, Jock, who's recently been rejected by his fraternity of choice. When the hammer of Jon's gun finally hits that solitary bullet, it sends the family over the edge of lunacy into the uncharted territory of honesty and reconciliation.

PLACE: A suburban American home.

TIME: The present.

JON. Some years ago, there was a robbery in this neighborhood. Do you remember?
[STEVE. Yeah, sure.]
JON. At the time, I bought a revolver, thinking, in case of an emergency, it might be a good thing to have around.
[ENID. Yes?]
JON. So I have this revolver. I hardly ever look at the thing, much less take it out of its box in my dresser. I have no particular affection for it. I'm not exactly a gun enthusiast. *(Steve puts down his drink.)* But the other day, three weeks ago actually, I decided to take a look at it. So I got the box out. This was … in the morning. You were asleep, honey. *(Enid nods.)* There was only one bullet in the box. Usually I have four. Don't ask me why. I just arbitrarily

decided on four bullets. But now there was only one. I don't know where the other bullets went. *(He looks up at Jock.)* I thought maybe you had found it and shot the other three off somewhere.

[JOCK. (Weakly.) No, Dad. No.]

JON. *(Jon takes out the gun.)* It doesn't matter at all. The thing was, I took the one bullet, and I went downstairs. *(He takes out a bullet. Springs open the gun.)* At first I thought it was impossible. Literally impossible. Which is something that fascinated me. It fascinated me more than anything I've ever seen or done or thought of in my entire life. The thought that I myself can do the impossible. The thought that all the millions of possibilities which are seething around and through my life are tangible — they are tangible, and I can reach out and grasp them, and hold them, and make them my own. The life that I have, that any of us has, seems like reality, but the fact is, there is no such thing as reality, reality is an arbitrary construct, and unless we empower it, it, in fact, ceases to exist. *(He puts the bullet into the gun and closes it. He smiles.)* And that makes me happy. *(He spins the cylinder and points the gun back toward the right side of his head. He pulls the trigger, and the gun goes off. Blackout.)*

THE RULES OF CHARITY

BY JOHN BELLUSO

MONTY — Loretta's father, handsome, very intelligent, late 40s, uses a wheelchair, has cerebral palsy but is only slightly speech impaired.

SYNOPSIS: Loretta thinks she is a machine. Her father, Monty, seeks independence and a place in history. Will Loretta learn the secret she needs to hear? Will Monty forgive her for a slap across the face that broke the rules? A play about the body, love and contradiction.

PLACE: A living room in an apartment and a single section of street. In the apartment, a couch, kitchen table, chairs, and a hospital-type bed. A front door, a door to a bedroom and a door to a kitchen.

TIME: The present.

MONTY. Yes. If I were born in ancient Greece, Sparta, with twisted legs, and a twisted spine. Children, babies who were born crippled and twisted in ancient Greece, in Sparta, they were taken to a place. *[LH. A place?]*
MONTY. A great section of earth was dug from the ground, a round ditch with a large stone in the middle of it. This was called "The Apothetai," which means "The Place of Exposure." *(Beat.)* My twisted naked body would be left on that stone, and those who brought me here would leave me on this rock, they would turn and walk away. *(Beat.)* I imagine I would be lying on this cold rock, and storms would come. *(Slowly pretending to die over the following.)* Dark storms, wind and rain. And my tiny body would wrestle and turn, and I would scream over the sounds of the wind. And somehow, I don't know how, but my newborn mouth would somehow find language. My tiny lips would open and softly whisper the words:
Isolation.
Isolation.
Isolation.
And that would be where my story would end. *(LH slowly*

approaches him. LH gently lifts his head.)
[LH. I didn't know, that things like that happened to people like
you —]
MONTY. People with disabled bodies have always existed, always, throughout history, but most people have no idea what their lives were like. It is an experience, which no one knows, or wants to know, the history of. *(Monty smiles at LH, lovingly.)* Thank you for listening to me.

THE SEAFARER

BY CONOR McPHERSON

MR. LOCKHART — An acquaintance of Nicky's, 50s.

SYNOPSIS: THE SEAFARER is a chilling play about the sea, Ireland, and the power of myth. It's Christmas Eve, and Sharky has returned to Dublin to look after his irascible, aging brother who's recently gone blind. Old drinking buddies Ivan and Nicky are holed up at the house too, hoping to play some cards. But with the arrival of a stranger from the distant past, the stakes are raised ever higher. Sharky may be playing for his very soul.

PLACE: The action takes place in a house in Baldoyle, a coastal settlement north of Dublin City. It is an old area which could hardly be called a town these days. It is rather a suburb of the city with a church and a few pubs and shops at its heart. From the coast here one is looking at the north side of the Howth peninsula. Howth Head (Binn Eadair) is a hill on the peninsula which marks the northern arm of Dublin Bay. Due to its prominence it has long been the focus of myths and legends.

TIME: Act Two takes place late on Christmas Eve night.

LOCKHART. What's hell? *(He gives a little laugh.)* Hell is … *(He stares gloomily.)* Well, you know, Sharky, when you're walking round and round the city and the street lights have all come on and it's cold. Or you're standing outside a shop where you were hanging around reading the magazines, pretending to buy one 'cause you've no money and nowhere to go and your feet are like blocks of ice in those stupid little slip-on shoes you bought for chauffeuring. And you see all the people who seem to live in another world all snuggled up together in the warmth of a tavern or a cosy little house, and you just walk and walk and walk and you're on your own and nobody knows who you are. And you're hoping you *won't* meet anyone you know because of the blistering shame that rises up in your face and you have to turn away because you know you can't even deal with the thought that someone might love you, because of all the pain you always cause. Well, that's a fraction of the self-loathing you feel in Hell, except it's worse. Because there truly is no-one to love you. You're locked in a space that's smaller than a coffin. And it's lying a thousand miles down, under the bed of a vast, icy, pitch-black sea. You're buried alive in there. And it's so cold that you don't even feel your angry tears freezing in your eyelashes and your very bones ache with deep perpetual agony and you think, "I must be going to die … " But you never die. You never even sleep because every few minutes you're gripped by a claustrophobic panic and you get so frightened you squirm uselessly against the stone walls and the heavy lid you've banged your head off a million times and your heart beats so fast against your ribs you think, "I *must* be going to die … " But of course … you never will. Because of what you did, and what you didn't do. *(Pause. Sharky stares into his bleak eternal fate.)* That's where I am, Sharky. I know you see me here in this man's clothes, but that's where I really am … Out on that sea. *(Short pause.)* Oh, you'd have loved heaven, Sharky. It's *unbelievable!* Time just slips away in heaven, Sharky. But not for you. No. You are about to find out that time is bigger and blacker and so much more boundless than you could ever have thought possible. *(Sharky looks down forlornly.)* Poor old Sharky. You've really got it for her, haven't you?

SEE ROCK CITY

BY ARLENE HUTTON

RALEIGH — In his 20s, raised on a sharecrop.

SYNOPSIS: Picking up a year after the ending of Last Train to Nibroc, *this tender and funny sequel follows May and Raleigh through the end of World War II. A medical condition keeps Raleigh from military service, and he is forced to sit idly on the porch, watching the cars drive by, as May supports them both as a high school principal. Faced with daily rejection letters for his writing, constant criticism from his mother and taunts of cowardice from townspeople, Raleigh fights to find meaning in his new life. When tragedy strikes the family and May loses her job to returning soldiers, she discovers she must make an unimaginable sacrifice to save her relationship with Raleigh. This tender portrayal of married life shows the best of the human spirit and its ability to overcome any obstacles.*

PLACE: The front porch of a modest bungalow in eastern Kentucky.

TIME: June 1944.

RALEIGH. You remember Dimwit Danny?
[MAY. Sure.]
RALEIGH. 'Member how he had that ole white mule? That ole white mule and a buckboard?
[MAY. What about it?]
RALEIGH. 'Member how Dimwit used to meet the train every day and carry people's luggage? He'd sit on the bench outside Stewie's, napping. That ole mule in the back, hitched to the buckboard? That mule would know exactly what time it was and just before the train was due would come 'round to the front of Stewie's and stand there in front of Dimwit Danny waitin' to go to the station and meet the train.
[MAY. I don't remember that.]
RALEIGH. Well, I sure do. That mule would stay in the back lot behind the store until he knew it was time to go meet the train.

[MAY. *My daddy's mules were never that smart.*]

RALEIGH. Well, one day, I take a bucket of black paint and a paintbrush and while Dimwit Danny is nappin' in out front of Stewie's I go around t' the back and paint black stripes on that ole white mule.

[MAY. *You do what?*]

RALEIGH. I paint black stripes on that old white mule.

[MAY. *Why on earth would you do a thing like that?*]

RALEIGH. Wanted to see what a zebra looked like.

[MAY. *A what?*]

RALEIGH. A zebra. In school we're reading all about Africa and I can't figure out what a zebra would look like. So I paint stripes on that ol' mule and then I stand back and look at it and I say to myself, well, so that's what a zebra looks like!

[MAY. *You didn't.*]

RALEIGH. Did, too. And my momma nearly whupped me for it.

[MAY. *I just bet she did. How'd she find out?*]

RALEIGH. Well, about the time I finish paintin' stripes on him, the mule knows it's time to wake up Dimwit to go meet the train, so that striped mule takes off headin' 'round to the front of Stewie's. And I follow after him because I want to imagine what a *moving* zebra looks like, with the stripes moving an' all. And ever'body on Main Street stops in their tracks when they see this zebra-striped mule and they laugh and point and laugh and Dimwit just can't figure out how his mule has stripes all of a sudden. Somebody sees me with the paint bucket and runs tells my daddy. Well, after supper my momma takes me to Dimwit's house — he lived with his sister — and my momma drags me up the steps and knocks on the door. When Dimwit opens it, my momma tells him that I have somethin' to say to him. So I tell Dimwit how I painted stripes on his mule because I wanted to see what a zebra looked like and that my momma is gonna whoop me for it. And Dimwit, he looks at me, and then he looks at my momma and he says to my momma that I didn't mean no harm. And for her not to punish me. And my momma has to promise that she won't lay a hand on me.

[MAY. *Reckon Dimwit wasn't such a dimwit after all.*]

A SMALL, MELODRAMATIC STORY

BY STEPHEN BELBER

PERRY — Male, 50, shy, black, strong, angry, tender.

SYNOPSIS: In Washington D.C., a widow named O is trying to fig-ure out whether life is worth re-engaging with. In her path are the 1968 riots, the first Gulf War, the Freedom of Information Act and herself. There's also an archivist named Keith, a cop named Perry and a kid named Cleo. And finally, there's the question of just how much about anything do we really need to know.

PLACE: Washington, D.C.

TIME: The present.

PERRY. *(Exploding.)* No, what's bullshit is you running around behind my back acting like Sherlock fucking Holmes!!! I don't need you so bad that I need you checking up on me, O! I ask you to trust me and you *stick* it in my face!!! And the thing is, I bet you don't feel any better right now than you did before you talked to him. Because I *know* you didn't walk out of there with an answer, I *know* that! — and the *reason* I know that is because there *is* none! The only *answer* is that I had to do something as a part of my job, and I didn't do it as perfectly as I was supposed to and maybe it ruined my career and a large part of my life, but I moved on and now I'm just trying to do my little thing, and then you walk in here fifteen years later and have the *nerve* to judge me, to *assume* something about me that you have no right at all to assume ... and you want me to say, "Oh, OK then, go ahead and tell me who I am, tell me how fucking racist and mean and wrong I am." Well you know what I say to that, O? — I say fuck you and get the fuck outta my house!

STRING FEVER

BY JACQUELYN REINGOLD

ARTIE — 60s. Lily's father. A retired salesman. Likes to talk. Talks fast and loud. Has a big heart.

SYNOPSIS: Lily juggles the big issues: turning forty, artificial insemi-nation and the elusive scientific Theory of Everything. Lily's world includes an Icelandic comedian, her wisecracking best friend, a cat-loving physicist, her no-longer-suicidal father and an ex-boyfriend who carries around a chair.

ARTIE. Well, I had some problems.
[MATTHEW. Really?]
ARTIE. Yeah, I uh put a knife in my chest.
[MATTHEW. Ow.]
ARTIE. Several times.
[MATTHEW. Wow.]
ARTIE. I wanted to die.
[MATTHEW. Yeah.]
ARTIE. But, hey, I couldn't even do that right.
[MATTHEW. Right.]
ARTIE. I mean what kind of life is this, I have to shit in a bag you know.
[MATTHEW. Yeah.]
ARTIE. I can't go out, I can't go twenty minutes without having to empty it. Of shit. Of my shit. Or gas. You wouldn't believe. It's constantly filling up with gas and shit.
[MATTHEW. Hmm.]
ARTIE. So I stuck a knife in my chest, right here. In my heart.
[MATTHEW. Yeah.]
ARTIE. Beverly came home and found me, bleeding all over. She had to buy a new mattress. Scrub the carpet. Everything.
[MATTHEW. Jeez.]
ARTIE. Called 911. The ambulance came. The police came. Pretty quickly. Read her her rights. 'Cause who knows, right, she could have done it. That happens. God knows that happens. So

they read her her rights. Miranda, like on TV, like bloody *Law and Order*. Then they helicopter me here. And I went into surgery.
[MATTHEW. Yeah.]
ARTIE. And this doctor, this Indian lady doctor, she fixed me up, right here, county hospital. I mean my insides had been put together with Gore-Tex but they were springing leaks, and no one could fix it. But now: no more bag.
[MATTHEW. Wow.]
ARTIE. That's something huh? *(Matthew nods.)* I had to try to kill myself to get my shit fixed.
[MATTHEW. Yeah.]
ARTIE. I've had, what, twenty surgeries in the last five years? You name it, I've had it. And then they told me not to eat for six months, I mean that was the one pleasure I had left. You wouldn't believe what my chest looks like. A road map. Of Los Angeles. With some of it made outta pigskin. I got pigskin. And I got no nipples. Swear to God. One day I coughed and my entire guts spilled out, that's when they put in the Gore-Tex. And then they had me on so many drugs I thought it was 1963. Throw in a breathing tube and some electroshock therapy, thirty-seven antidepressants, and you'll get just a little part of this picture. Hell, you think doctors know what they're doing, that they're experts, that medicine's a science — till you spend as much time in hospitals as I have. Then you realize it's an art. That's right. And just think of all the bad art that's out there. All the terrible terrible art. Most of those doctors are as stupid as the rest of us. But at least I can sit on the goddamn toilet now. Or I will be able to — soon. I mean I got so many problems inside of me it could not last, you know, the connection, but for now it should be all right. 'Cause of that Indian lady doctor. An artist. Van Gogh. Rembrandt. Picasso.
[MATTHEW. That's great.]
ARTIE. And you know why I didn't die?
[MATTHEW. No.]
ARTIE. I stabbed myself in the chest quite a few times. With a knife — this big. A chef's knife. And I didn't die. You wanna know why?
[MATTHEW. Why?]
ARTIE. The only reason is 'cause I've had so much surgery that my heart is wrapped in scar tissue. How do you like that?

THE SUNSET LIMITED

BY CORMAC McCARTHY

BLACK — 30s/40s.

SYNOPSIS: On a subway platform in New York City, an ex-con from the South saves the life of an intellectual atheist who wasn't looking for salvation. Now, the reformed murderer-turned-savior ventures to offer salvation of another kind. The two men are named Black and White, as indeed they are. White is disillusioned and disenchanted by the modern world. Black had an epiphany after a nasty knife fight in the penitentiary and discovered a faith that he now wants to share with others, or at least with White. Black begins in control, but it quickly becomes clear that the non-believer is much more secure in his convictions than the believer. Is Black a guardian angel or just a sinner looking for redemption?

PLACE: A room in a tenement building in a black ghetto in New York City.

BLACK. All right. I'm in the chowline and I'm gettin my chow and this nigger in the line behind me gets into it with the server. Says the beans is cold and he throws the ladle down in the beans. And when he done that they was beans splashed on me. Well, I wasnt goin to get into it over some beans but it did piss me off some. I'd just put on a clean suit — you know, khakis, shirt and trousers — and you only got two a week. And I did say somethin to him like Hey man, watch it, or somethin like that. But I went on, and I'm thinkin, just let it go. Let it go. And then this dude says somethin to me and I turned and looked back at him and when I done that he stuck a knife in me. I never even seen it. And the blood is just flyin. And this aint no jailhouse shiv neither. It's one of them Italian switchblades. One of them black and silver jobs. And I didnt do a thing in the world but duck and step under the rail and I reached and got hold of the leg of this table and it come off in my hand just as easy. And it's got this big long screw stickin out of the end of it and I went to wailin on this nigger's head and I didnt quit. I beat on it till you couldnt hardly tell it was a head. And that screw'd stick in his head and I'd have to stand on him to pull it out again.

THE SUNSET LIMITED

BY CORMAC McCARTHY

WHITE — Middle-aged.

SYNOPSIS: On a subway platform in New York City, an ex-con from the South saves the life of an intellectual atheist who wasn't looking for salvation. Now, the reformed murderer-turned-savior ventures to offer salvation of another kind, bringing the failed suicide victim back to his Harlem apartment for an articulate and moving debate about truth, fiction and belief. The two men are named Black and White, as indeed they are. White is disillusioned and disenchanted by the modern world. Black had an epiphany after a nasty knife fight in the penitentiary and discovered a faith that he now wants to share with others, or at least with White. Black begins in control, but it quickly becomes clear that White is much more secure in his convictions than the believer. And when White goes on the attack, his nihilism steamrolls his opponent. Was White really saved, or is he stuck in a kind of purgatory?

PLACE: A room in a tenement building in a black ghetto in New York City.

WHITE. *(Coldly.)* I dont believe in God. Can you understand that? Look around you man. Cant you see? The clamor and din of those in torment has to be the sound most pleasing to his ear. And I loathe these discussions. The argument of the village atheist whose single passion is to revile endlessly that which he denies the existence of in the first place. Your fellowship is a fellowship of pain and nothing more. And if that pain were actually collective instead of simply reiterative then the sheer weight of it would drag the world from the walls of the universe and send it crashing and burning through whatever night it might yet be capable of engendering until it was not even ash. And justice? Brotherhood? Eternal life? Good god, man. Show me a religion that prepares one for death. For nothingness. There's a church I might enter. Yours prepares one only for more life. For dreams and illusions and lies. If you could banish the fear of death from men's hearts they wouldnt live a day.

Who would want this nightmare if not for fear of the next? The shadow of the axe hangs over every joy. Every road ends in death. Or worse. Every friendship. Every love. Torment, betrayal, loss, suffering, pain, age, indignity, and hideous lingering illness. All with a single conclusion. For you and for every one and every thing that you have chosen to care for. There's the true brotherhood. The true fellowship. And everyone is a member for life. You tell me that my brother is my salvation? My salvation? Well then damn him. Damn him in every shape and form and guise. Do I see myself in him? Yes. I do. And what I see sickens me. Do you understand me? *Can* you understand me? *(The black sits with his head lowered.)* I'm sorry.

tempODYSSEY

BY DAN DIETZ

DEAD BODY BOY — 20s.

SYNOPSIS: "It wasn't me. It was the black hole." With these words, a temp worker named Genny launches us on an epic, fantastical journey through corporate America, Appalachia, astrophysics and beyond. TEMPODYSSEY tells the story of a young woman who's convinced she's the goddess of death. Fleeing the imminent creation of a black hole on one side of the country, she lands smack in the middle of a bomb manufacturing company on the other. Her only hope lies in the unlikely guise of a nameless temp, Dead Body Boy who considers himself immortal. Can he help Genny cast off her dark mythology once and for all? Or will she explode, taking all of downtown Seattle with her?

PLACE: A very tall office building smack in the middle of downtown Seattle.

(Dead Body Boy is finishing his smoke.)

DEAD BODY BOY. So I guess it's no surprise I went into office work. I was raised to make order out of chaos. And I know how to let one crucial little thread go and watch the whole thing unravel. Just in case they ever think they don't need you.

I'm a temp who's sort of gone over to the other side. No, strike that. I'm balanced between this side and the other. I hover like a buddha at the top of a needle peak and though the wind may roar I keep steady and still and … um … so anyway, they keep wanting me to come on permanent. They say they can't afford to keep paying my temp salary like this, but when I say no, they say, well, stay one more month. Month after month after month.

The other employees eye me suspiciously. Some of them are temps who went over. And they say things like: The Benefits are better, you get to go on Company Outings, why are you still a temp? But they know why. And it eats them up.

I am the Unattainable. I am the thing you love because it won't ever quite surrender. Because it won't be dominated. I will do everything for you except Be Yours. And that is the secret of joy in this life. I know that as soon as I lean too far in one direction or the other, I'll vanish. If I care too much about this place, go permanent: POOF! I disappear into the rows of cubicles, just another carpal tunnel case. If I care too little: POOF! I'm replaceable, I'm just another temp, I'm outta here. Balance is like, all.

Some people go into temping to disappear. I went into temping to stick in the eyes of everyone here. The CEO knows my name, pops by my cubicle every once in a while, waggles his cashmere tongue. He calls me The Holdout, The One With Balls. There've been whispers about hiring me direct into a VeePee slot.

Which of course I'd never take. I'm more powerful than any VeePee in this building.

WHITE PEOPLE

BY J.T. ROGERS

MARTIN BAHMUELLER — Around 50.

SYNOPSIS: Now — right now — what does it mean to be a white American? What does it mean for any American to live in a country that is not the one you were promised? WHITE PEOPLE is a controversial and darkly funny play about the lives of three ordinary Americans placed under the spotlight: Martin, a Brooklyn-born high powered attorney for a white-shoe law firm in St. Louis; Mara Lynn, a housewife and former homecoming queen in Fayetteville, NC; and Alan, a young professor struggling to find his way in New York City. Through heart-wrenching confessions, they wrestle with guilt, prejudice, and the price they and their children must pay for their actions.

PLACE: Martin's office on the waterfront in downtown St. Louis, Missouri.

TIME: Now. Sunday.

MARTIN. Yes, fine: I'm the asshole! But this is not fun, it is work. That is why it is called a job, which comes from "Job," which means "to suffer." But that's different from being mean. That's different from being unfair. I know my reputation here. I am not an ignorant man. I can read the bathroom walls. The black employees of this firm do not like me. Not all, but many. That's fine. To be liked is not why I am being paid. Being liked did not bring me halfway across the country to shake up this firm. What did was understanding the responsibility of my actions. I am in charge here because I understand the rules.

This is business. In America, in business, this is how we dress, this is how we talk. Seal of approval. You go down to fifteen, take a left to the mail room, every person working there is black. Oh, we're not supposed to talk about that but this is reality. This is truth. They work here, they are part of this community, and a community has rules. I took this position, I made changes. I don't want to see gold teeth. I don't want to see your butt cheeks hanging out of your pants. See people dressed like hoods, like killers. Oh! I know! I know! I've heard it all before: It's just an "image," it's a "style" thing. Can we stop and use our rational minds for a moment? What style is being promoted? What image is being sent to the world? What if I walked in here, nine A.M. tomorrow, white hood over my head?

"Oh, it's just an image. It's just my style."

And then! Then there's the whole music thing. Oh, boy. I try to be a hip guy. I try to be with it. You want a radio on your desk in the mail room? Knock yourself out. But now what you *play* on that radio, that's my bone of contention. All this hip-hopping-crotch-grabbing-bang-bang … Whatever! You can't play it for your mother, don't play it in here. Now hold on! It's not like I listen to Tommy Dorsey. But *please!* Wax out of your ears and listen to what they are saying! These words! Lyrics — lyrics like:

Bitch, bitch, bitch.

Yo, yo, yo.

I got a big dick, I got a big dick,

Whoo!

That is not funny. I have a daughter. The women who work here, they are somebody's daughter. Raping them, cutting them up, set to music? That is not music. That is hateful. What possible right is there to be so hateful? And don't come to me with "Back Then." Don't give me that "Sins of the Forefathers" mumbo jumbo. What, because things happened to people's grandparents, now they have special rights? This releases them from responsibility? Grandpa was responsible for his actions, us for ours. The past is past. Do not look to history for an excuse.

Steven tries the same thing with me. Sees what music he can get away with. He knows the garbage I won't let him play in the house. If anything, his is worse. These people can't even keep a beat, for God's sake. Bunch of Tourette's victims bouncing around with their heads shaved. I say:

"Steven, are you listening? Are you listening to the words?"

He just glares at the floor. Glares at it like he's trying to burn a hole straight through. Hunched over, moving the zipper on his jacket up and down. Not a word. Just like always. I'm watching Steven, head-phones on, cutting me out, thrashing about. I am watching my son.

Where does this anger come from?

PERMISSIONS ACKNOWLEDGMENTS

100 SAINTS YOU SHOULD KNOW by Kate Fodor. Copyright © 2008, Kate Fodor. Reprinted by permission of Val Day, William Morris Endeavor Entertainment, 1325 Avenue of the Americas, New York, NY 10019 on the author's behalf.

THE ACTION AGAINST SOL SCHUMANN by Jeffery Sweet. Copyright © 2003, Jeffrey Sweet. Reprinted by permission of Susan Schulman, Susan Schulman Agency, 454 West 44th Street, New York, NY 10036 on the author's behalf.

THE AGONY & THE AGONY by Nicky Silver. Copyright © 2008, Nicky Silver. Reprinted by permission of John Buzzetti, the Gersh Agency, 41 Madison Avenue, New York, NY 10010 on the author's behalf.

ALL THAT I WILL EVER BE by Alan Ball, Copyright © 2008, Alan Ball. Reprinted by permission of Peter Hagan, Abrams Artists Agency, 275 Seventh Avenue, New York, NY 10001 on the author's behalf.

ALL THE RAGE by Keith Reddin. Copyright © 2007, Keith Reddin. Reprinted by permission of Mary Harden, Harden-Curtis Associates, 850 Seventh Avenue, New York, NY 10019 on the author's behalf.

ALMOST BLUE by Keith Reddin. Copyright © 2007, Keith Reddin. Reprinted by permission of Mary Harden, Harden-Curtis Associates, 850 Seventh Avenue, New York, NY 10019 on the author's behalf.

ANNA IN THE TROPICS by Nilo Cruz. Copyright © 2003, Nilo Cruz. Reprinted by permission of Peregrine Whittlesey, Peregrine Whittlesey Agency, 279 Central Park West, New York, NY 10024 on the author's behalf.

BEAUTIFUL CHILD by Nicky Silver. Copyright © 2004, Nicky Silver. Reprinted by permission of John Buzzetti, the Gersh Agency, 41 Madison Avenue, New York, NY 10010 on the author's behalf.

BLACK SHEEP by Lee Blessing. Copyright © 2003, Lee Blessing. Reprinted by permission of Judy Boals, Judy Boals Inc., 307 West 38th Street, New York, NY 10018 on the author's behalf.

BOYS AND GIRLS by Tom Donaghy. Copyright © 2003, Tom Donaghy. Reprinted by permission of International Creative Management, 825 Eighth Avenue, New York, NY 10019 on the author's behalf.

BUG by Tracy Letts. Copyright © 2005, Tracy Letts. Reprinted by permission of Ron Gwiazda, Abrams Artists Agency, 275 Seventh Avenue, New York, NY 10001 on the author's behalf.